SpringerBriefs in Business

More information about this series at http://www.springer.com/series/8860

Ermelinda Kordha Tolica • Kozeta Sevrani
Klodiana Gorica

Information Society Development through ICT Market Strategies

Albania versus Other Developing Countries

 Springer

Ermelinda Kordha Tolica
Department of Business Administration
University of Vlora "Ismail Qemali"
Vlore, Albania

Klodiana Gorica
Department of Marketing
University of Tirana
Tirana, Albania

Kozeta Sevrani
Department of Mathematics, Statistics,
 and Applied Informatics
University of Tirana
Tirana, Albania

ISSN 2191-5482   ISSN 2191-5490   (electronic)
SpringerBriefs in Business
ISBN 978-3-319-17195-1   ISBN 978-3-319-17196-8   (eBook)
DOI 10.1007/978-3-319-17196-8

Library of Congress Control Number: 2015937623

Springer Cham Heidelberg New York Dordrecht London

Printed on acid-free paper

Springer International Publishing AG Switzerland is part of Springer Science+Business Media
(www.springer.com)

REPUBLIC OF ALBANIA
ACADEMY OF SCIENCES PRESIDENCY

Tirana, 19 March 2015

In today's world, information is one of the most important elements that has impacted the development of markets, economies, and societies. Information society, e-readiness, and ICT sector are concepts that have been the argument of a lot of studies, papers, and books in the last decade. Developed countries as well as developing ones are involved in the discussions, because they have realized the importance that information has for development.

The monograph that is presented here by three university professors is the result of their continuous work in the field of ICT and ICT market, especially in their application in Albania. In this book, the reader can find a thorough analysis of the relationship between important elements dealing with information society development. The elements in the new scheme have been separately explained by different authors and/or institutions. But the way that they interact with each other is a new proposal by the authors.

Another strong point of this study is the comparative analyses between SEE countries, giving an overview of the region. The focus on ICT market gives also an important element for the development of information society. The factors that have to be taken into account for strategy development in the national and industry level are described, by the new model proposed.

This book can be very useful for those not only in the academic field but also in the private sector and public policy. Professionals in the ICT field may look at the development of their products and services in a different perspective depending on the model described.

Academic Prof. Dr. Gudar Beqiraj
Vice-President
Address: Sheshi "Fan S. Noli"
Tirana, Albania
Mob: 00 355 68 20 16 630
e-mail: gudar.beqiraj@yahoo.com

REPUBLIC OF ALBANIA
UNIVERSITY OF TIRANA
FACULTY OF ECONOMY

Review for the MONOGRAPH:

"Information Society Development Through ICT Market Strategies: Albania vs. Other Developing Countries," with authors: ERMELINDA KORDHA, KOZETA SEVRANI, KLODIANA GORICA.

Society is ringing the changes due to the expansion of the digital-oriented environment and ecosystem helping out the information to be widespread. It is strongly affirmed that "Information is Power" in terms of understanding the problems, in terms of deriving solutions, and in terms of advocating where, how, and when decision-makers need to act. Also, information development relates too much and enhances a new interface with the marketing strategies.

In this regard, the spread of Information and Communication Technologies (ICT) through market strategies has become very important due to economic and businesses development. Governments, professionals in the field of ICT, marketers, economists, and businesses need to draft and develop strategies to outdistance not only in the working environment but also in the society as a whole. ICTs throughout the last decade have served as a catalyst for development, fostering new ways of introducing innovation to the business industry.

This monograph is a reflection of such a reality in developing countries like Albania where the need of building up a standardized information flow system is of a high significance.

1. First, it fulfills the need of a professional audience, related to information and marketing also, into the new sector that is offering products and services of ICT in the individual and massive business markets.
2. Second, the material may be very useful to academics for further research in this field and to students, who may broaden a strong body of fundamental knowledge, necessary for their studies.
3. Third, it lies and covers both disciplines, information and marketing, and brings a new study for Albanian Market.
4. While last but not least, businesses and organizations may find ideas for growing further their technological prospective.

The value added comes from a fine style and a proper monograph structuring, which makes it flow toward the final goal of recommending the right path for ICT development in Albania, compared with other developing countries. After all, it is the future of business communication that we are all looking toward.

Prof. Dr. Ilia KRISTO
Lecturer: International Business & Marketing
University of Tirana
Faculty of Economics
Mob: 00355673386842
e-mail: ilia.kristo@yahoo.com

REPUBLIC OF ALBANIA
UNIVERSITY OF TIRANA
FACULTY OF ECONOMY

Review for the MONOGRAPH:

"Information Society Development Through ICT Market Strategies: Albania vs. Other Developing Countries"

The monograph at hand is an important study of a field that is growing rapidly, marketing and ITs, not only in developed countries but also in developing countries such as Albania. It comes out of the need to acquire more knowledge about the different factors that are affecting the development of new marketing strategies of the society as a result of ITs, resulting in a new phase.

The value of this study remains in the new point of view of ITs as an industrial sector in Albania, studying the elements that interrelate for Information Society development, for the whole market strategies, from e-readiness to IT strategy and its actors.

The aim of the authors in this work is really important because of the value it brings to readers of different categories, such as students, professors, and professionals in the field, but over all decision-makers of business, organizations, and government.

The comparative analyses with other developing countries give the study the needed illustration of the latest developments and the differences that exist in the region that is struggling to achieve sustainable development.

The structure of the book gives clearly a logical flow from the principles of building the information society to the impact of the ICT sector for its construction. I evaluate as a very useful resource for all categories of academics in the field of information and marketing, even management, students, etc.

Based on the above considerations, I fully support this publication.

Prof. Dr. Fatmir MEMAJ
Deputy Dean
University of Tirana
Faculty of Economy
Mob: +355692095495
e-mail: fatmirmemaj@feut.edu.al

Abstract

Information has become an important element without which society cannot achieve its objectives. The term "information society" is increasingly used nowadays because of the importance and necessity of information in today's dynamic environment. Organization for Economic Cooperation and Development (OECD) notes that information infrastructures are expected to stimulate economic growth, increase productivity, create jobs, and improve on the quality of life (Gichoya 2005). National economies are increasingly tightly tied together globally by ultra high-speed information networks (Jun-Hwan Kim 2000).

It is for these reasons that many studies state that the role of ICTs as enablers of sustainable development is growing. The overall goal of this work is to give a special approach to information society development through a strategy for ICT sector growth, studying a developing country like Albania, where we can see the proper illustration.

The first step of this research is to show the importance of studying ICTs in the light of building an information society. In fact, the efforts of a country to build an information society, in order to benefit in terms of sustainable development, are closely related to the efforts of building strong information infrastructures and a growing ICT sector. Many indicators related to information society measurement deal in fact with the infrastructures needed and the products and services of ICT sector.

But, failure to submit ICT in contexts, which are contrary to techno-economic rationality, is reflected in many cases in developing countries. Thus, a defining characteristic of this research is to understand the contexts that confront ICT and information systems development in developing countries in terms of their conditions. In fact, the development of ICT sector is driven by different forces, depending also on the political, economic, and social conditions of each country, counting on public and private efforts. The strategy for building an information society must count on these forces, as well as on the frame for measuring the readiness of this society to enter in the information and electronic age. That is why this book will summarize and categorize all the factors affecting ICT sector growth, illustrating with the situation of information society and the development of ICT sector in Albania and other developing countries in the South East Europe (SEE).

   The investment in infrastructures is in fact the first important step to Information Society development, so the strategy for ICT sector growth depends heavily on it, in its first steps. Management for speed, quality, and access to a variability of services will guide the implementation for the right policies. New emerging technologies, such as broadband, wireless networks, and cloud computing, are always changing the environment of ICT sector and the infrastructures used. Financial forces and investments are playing an important role when speaking about the further development and growth of ICT sector. But the future challenge, especially for developing countries will be the decision to count more on public policies, inciting the ICT sector or the private investments oriented through more services and infrastructures for developing successfully an information society.

Contents

About the Authors

Klodiana Gorica, Vice Dean in Faculty of Economy, University of Tirana, is a Professor in Marketing and Tourism Department. She is Editorial Board member in many international well-known research journals, guest speaker, and member of many international conferences and symposiums, participating also in national and international projects. She is author/coauthor of many books, scientific articles abroad, and has participated in many international conferences. Her research interest include: entrepreneurial marketing, e-marketing, principles of marketing, sustainable tourism, tourism marketing.

Ermelinda Kordha is actually teaching at Business Administration Department, University "Ismail Qemali" of Vlora, since 1999. She actually teaches Management Information Systems and Marketing Research. The research work includes the participation in more than 20 International Conferences, inside and outside Albania as well as the publishing of over 12 articles in well-known International Journals. This is the result of her professional experience enriched from the implementation of different projects for community development and also the participation as an expert in research and analyses for EU projects.

Kozeta Sevrani is a Professor of Computer Science and Management Information Systems, and Head of the Department of Mathematics, Statistics, and Applied Informatics, at the Faculty of Economy, University of Tirana, Albania. Her research interests include: digital divide; issues and solutions in building information infrastructure, e-business, e-learning, and e-government in developing countries, particularly in Albania. She is the Editorial Board of several international journals and does an extended work in consulting private companies and government agencies in Albania. Also, she has presented her work in numerous national and international conferences. Her work has been published in several journals and she has co-authored four books.

Introduction

The importance of information is rising in societies around the world. Today, information has become an important element without which society actors as well as business cannot achieve their goals. The term "information society" is increasingly used nowadays instead of the terms "production" or "consumption society" because of the importance and necessity of information in today's dynamic environment. So, the society has entered in the stage of information society, in which the creation and dissemination of information processing has become the most significant economic activity and cultural development. An "information society" is a society in which we take for granted the role of information as it pervades and dominates the activities of government, business, and everyday life. The information society will be characterized by the fact that the rapid and convenient delivery of needed information is the ordinary state of affairs (Garfield 2001).

Along with the information society is born the Information Economy, in which knowledge is the main source of value. It characterizes an economy with an increased emphasis on informational activities and information industry. Problems appear already at the definition of information society or information economy (Karvalics 2005). The term "information economy" refers to "a new global electronic structure, wherein the production of information goods and services dominates wealth and job creation, and is underpinned by the use of information and communication technologies (ICTs) and the global information infrastructure." (Cogburn 1999). However, information economy is considered a "stage" of an economy, coming after manufacturing. Information society is a closely related but wider concept. Closer terms to information economy would include knowledge economy and postindustrial economy. Information and knowledge are the bedrock of the Knowledge Economy—the "currency" of modern societies (Markle Foundation 2003). The term "Knowledge Society" generally refers to a society, where knowledge is the primary production resource instead of capital and labor. Various observers describe today's global economy as one in transition to a "knowledge economy," as an extension of an "information society."

The terms "information economy" or "knowledge economy" have been mainstream in the business sector since the 1990s. The uninterrupted high economic productivity in the USA during the late 1990s was attributed to the new ICTs and their impact on business (Gurumurthy and Singh 2005). The public policy angle that the USA saw in these developments was to advocate a Global Information Infrastructure,[1] which will set the basics for "the networked economy," from the technological aspect. Europeans, on the other hand, popularized the term "information society."

In these conditions, ICTs are changing almost every sector of society and economy. Yet ICTs can be seen as tools, which value depends on implementation. Nowadays, ICTs can be applied to a tremendously diverse range of human experience. They are transforming virtually every sector of society and the economy. Today's technological transformations are intertwined with globalization, and together they are creating the new realities of the global economy.

There are many definitions of ICTs. They have their specifications according to different countries or organizations that are interested in the issuance of these definitions internationally.

"Information and communication technologies or ICTs include any device or application by entering here: radio, television, cell phones, computers, networking hardware and software, satellite systems and so forth, as well as various services and applications such as video conferences and distance learning." Usually, the term ICT is used in a particular context as ICT in education, health, governance, books, etc. This term is more common in Europe. More about ICT definition will be commented in the first chapter of this work.

In a society where the information and knowledge are of vital importance for the purpose of development, the role of ICT is growing. So, ICTs play the role of an enabler of development in several respects, cross-sector productivity and economic growth, specific social development goals and political participation and good governance, taking the society in the phase of information society.

However, the information society development is also connected with some concerns and threats (Castells 1996, 1997, 1998). Social conflicts and unrest look a bit different from what they used to be. They primarily stem from a lack of access to ICT and the skills required using it and, as a consequence, leading to the so-called digital divide of the society. It is believed that societies which lag behind in terms of the technological development are going to be isolated and excluded from the economic, social, and other types of activities (Cellary 2002). It may even be assumed that the digital exclusion in the nearest future will be equivalent to the social and economic exclusion of individuals, organizations as well as entire regions and societies.

Heeks (2002) observes that there is a big difference between ICT implementation and use between developed and developing countries. However, Westrup (2002) observes that similarities can also be expected. The difference is how problems are addressed in different countries.

That is why countries are especially concerned with the implementation of the right strategies for supporting information societies. Different initiatives, as United

---

[1] http://www.eff.org/Infrastructure/Govt_docs/gii_co-op_iitf.agenda

Nations as well as European countries initiatives, try to give orientations about ICT use in building information societies. So, according to European Commission, the importance of ICTs lies less on the technology itself than in its ability to create greater access to information and communication in communities with few services. Many countries have set up organizations for the promotion of ICT. If the less technologically developed countries were not given the opportunity of reaching developed areas, the growth of technological developments in the developed nations will only serve to increase the already existing economic space between these areas. To international level, the United Nations actively promote ICT for development as a means of reducing the digital divide.

A central role of markets and the private sector in the ICT was also advocated on the strength of another important argument that the new technology breakthroughs had been made possible singularly because of private sector innovation (Gurumurthy and Singh 2005). As ICTs became more important for the societies, all social and public matters are more dependent from the development of the private sector, which claims to be the leader in the technology field. The private sector in fact began to play a major role in areas that usually were administered by policies of local and central governments as well as different public institutions. Another important aspect where the private sector began to impact continuously the ways of interaction between government and citizens through the technology services offered to public institutions.

The development and the further use of ICTs, the impact of these trends in the economic development of countries, as well as in the interaction between private and public sector raised also the need for information society statistics and measurements. After the broad definitions of ICTs, the next steps in developing statistics for the information society/information economy is thus to develop a definition of ICT Commodities and a definition of the content industries.

Concerning the commodity definition of ICT goods and services, Eurostat undertook to lead and coordinate European work on a commodity classification, since 1998. Denmark participated and represented the Nordic ICT sector project under the aegis of the Council of Nordic Ministers. The USA coordinated North American work and Canada maintained a link between the North American and the European activities. Other participants included Australia, France, Korea, and the UK. Different initiatives continued by OECD and other organizations as the reader would have the opportunity to read in the second section of this work. But all of them tried to capture the rapid developments in these technologies, and represent them in an appropriate definition of ICT sector for the purpose of building information societies throughout the countries (OECD 2009).

The starting point for the definition of ICT in terms of activities and commodities, respectively, was to consider a number of broader issues associated with the delineation of the ICT sector, hopefully leading to the compilation of internationally comparable ICT sector statistics. But it was also said that some issues of detail about precisely which parts of an industry are to be included can only be settled when the definition of the goods and services has been completed.

So, an important aspect of the information society development in a country is the development of ICT sector in that country. This definition includes the ICT commodities and services. The definition of this sector and the importance of managing its different aspects for the purpose of developing proper strategies in the efforts of building the information society is further developed in Chap. 2.

This section is followed by a full representation of the data for Albania as one of the developing countries in the South East Europe (SEE) region. In this context, Albania is trying to give the proper importance and emphasis to, not just the use of information, but to the use of tools and technologies that enable efficiency in the collection, storage, processing, and distribution of data and the use of information. The Republic of Albania sees ICT development as an essential tool in building an information society, which in turn is fundamental to the rapid development of Albania and the region. Human capital is seen as the main source for the creation of information society in Albania, so, the application of ICT.

Thus, ICTs are finding today in the Albanian society, a steadily increasing use. For this reason albanian government has established and implemented the National Strategy for Information and communciation Technologies. The ICT national strategy is implemented since 2003 through different initiatives from public and private sector. The final goal is to impact in building the information society in Albania.

But which are the factors that impact the most the ICT sector development? These factors and forces are the following step of this work, in trying to fulfill the goal of building the proper strategies in the ICT sector. Public policies and private actions should not be limited to ICT definitions, or to the measurement of the statistics of ICT development, or information society development. This work brings to the reader the attention for the measurement of the most important indicators of ICT sector as part of the information society statistics, as well as all the forces that drive the sector development. Statistics of information society, e-readiness measurement, and other statistics of ICT sector in Albania will help in evaluating the development of ICT in our country. What is new here is a model that tries to include all these factors and further statistical analyses of data that will include the most important variables and factors, affecting the performance and the growth of the ICT sector in building the information society in Albania.

Questions raised in this book:

1. *What is the information society and what are the concepts underlying this new trend in the world economy?*
2. *What is the role of ICT sector and ICT infrastructures for the increasing use of ICT and building the information society in developed and developing countries?*
3. *How an ICT strategy is related to ICT sector—through the need for infrastructure and services?*
4. *How can different forces be analyzed together in a model of ICT sector growth for the purpose of facilitating the development and implementation of proper strategies, leading to information society development?*

5. *Should the public investment have the major importance, or should the private sector make the difference?*
6. *How should the experience of Albania as a developing country help other countries in developing the right strategies for Information Society development?*

Chapter 1
Information Society and the Efforts for an ICT Strategy

When we talk about the new information based economy, we're talking about a world in which people work with their brains instead of their hand, a world in which communications technology creates global competition—not just for running shoes and laptop computers, but also for bank loans and other services that can't be packed into a crate and shipped. We are in fact speaking of a world in which innovation is more important than mass production, investment buys new concepts or the means to create them, rather than new machines, a world in which rapid change is a constant, a world so different its emergence can only be described as a revolution.[1]

Information and communications technology or **information and communication technology**, usually abbreviated as **ICT**, is often used as an extended synonym for information technology (IT), but is usually a more general term that stresses the role of unified communications and the integration of telecommunications (telephone lines and wireless signals), computers, middleware as well as necessary software, storage, and audio–visual systems, which enable users to create, access, store, transmit, and manipulate information.[2] In other words, ICT consists of IT as well as telecommunication, broadcast media, all types of audio and video processing, and transmission and network-based control and monitoring functions. The expression was first used in 1997 in a report by Dennis Stevenson to the UK government and promoted by the new National Curriculum documents for the UK in 2000.

The term *ICT* is now also used to refer to the merging (convergence) of audio–visual and telephone networks with computer networks through a single cabling or link system. There are large economic incentives (huge cost savings due to elimination of the telephone network) to merge the audio–visual, building management, and telephone network with the computer network system using a single unified system of cabling, signal distribution, and management. This in turn has spurred the growth of organizations with the term ICT in their names to indicate their specialization in the process of merging the different network systems.

---

[1] *Wired magazine's*, *Encyclopedia of the New Economy http://hotwired.wired.com/special/ene/*
[2] According to the Online Oxford Dictionary

© The Author(s) 2015

E. Kordha Tolica et al., *Information Society Development through ICT Market Strategies*, SpringerBriefs in Business, DOI 10.1007/978-3-319-17196-8_1

According to Statistics Canada's Authority, ICT includes technologies such as desktop and laptop computers, software, peripheral equipment, and Internet connection aimed to meet the information processing and communication functions. ICT can also be defined as research or business development and technology use to process information and target communication.

The realization of new era information-based economy underscores the fact that ICTs have become a very important part of and drives the direction of the contemporary economy of the world. In using ICT and especially the Internet, many organizations have looked to add more value to the tangible products they sell, by providing additional information-based services. These can include online support, order tracking, order history, etc. Many of these initiatives focus on deepening the relationship with customers and suppliers. Others have moved their trading platform either partially or entirely onto the Internet. Using e-procurement, companies permit their customers to "empower" their employees to make purchases websites of noncore, low value, with them managing the total process, including establishing purchasing controls. These purchasing control rules cover specific pricing, spending limits, bearing the ordering of particular products, cost codes, blanket orders, and order passwords.

The twenty-first century is a period of economic, social, and technological transformations that facilitate development of the new society that is referred to as the information society (Bell 1973; Drucker 1993; Toffler 1980). The very notion of the information society was firstly used in 1960s by the Japanese economist Tadao Umesao. Different authors point out the impact that information technology has in the development of societies in all their dimensions. Literature also gives different interpretations of the information society term. For research purposes, it is assumed that the information society is some society whose development is largely determined by utilization of information and knowledge and by different information and communications technologies. It is believed that in case of the information society, information is a fundamental resource and the national income generating source (Olszak and Ziemba 2008).

The term "information economy" refers to "a new global electronic structure, wherein the production of information goods and services dominates wealth and job creation, and is underpinned by the use of information and communication technologies (ICTs) and the global information infrastructure." (Cogburn 1999).

Different computer-related technologies, including the hardware or software, wireless communications and the Internet, microprocessors, biotechnologies, in general, information technologies, are intensively being offered in a society, which is more and more dependent on these technologies. The characteristic methods which are inexpensive for storing, transferring, and processing of vast amounts of information (by means of data bases, data warehouses, knowledge repositories, etc.) result in creating new conditions for effective communications, especially in running business activities in a partial or even complete different model, as well as individuals in learning and acquiring more knowledge and capabilities through the use of technology.

It is necessary to note that in the information society context, economy is not simply continuation of already existing methods to be used while producing goods and rendering services. Universal usage of different information and communications media along with sophisticated electronic information resources that are available to all citizens involves major changes in lifestyles, work habits, and business manners (Mansell and Steinmuller 2000). It is preferred to use a principle dealing with network cooperation. So, organizations and their customers can experience a lot of business processes through e-business, e-commerce, and virtual organizations. Economic processes are realized on electronic platforms and human beings are more and more frequently excluded.

It is clearly noticed, when analyzing the nature of the information society, that its typical characteristic is the demand for new professions and specialties in the field of nonmaterial activities, mainly services, related, first of all, to information processing in broad terms. Let us remember here that in the earlier forms of the civilization development, e.g., during the agrarian phase of development, such professions as a fisherman, a hunter, and a farmer dominated are required, while in the industrial phase—the professions related to the manufacturing process are more important. While in the information phase of the society development required professions include information intermediaries, electronic market makers, webmasters, Internet service providers, information and knowledge brokers. At the same time, we can see a dramatic reduction in employment in the area of material production, both industrial and agricultural. Professional work increasingly tends to be not connected with fixed employment. Owing to ICT, work may be done at home or in any other place and time. Work is becoming personalized and nonformal. At the same time, people often have to retrain, change their jobs, or even professions (Olszak et al. 2009).

On the other hand, firms across the economic landscape, including those in developing countries, will need to learn how to acquire and use information effectively if they hope to succeed in today's increasingly integrated global economy. In many cases, information strategies are communicated just as information society development programs, with direct concentration of governmental resources and systematic realization of long-term operative programs (Karvalics 1997). In visioning and in developing ICT strategies, it is important to think strategically of ICTs as enablers of human development. It is imperative to consider how enhanced access to information can improve the lives of people as well as stimulate the economy and streamline government.

While there are good grounds for believing that the use of ICTs are positively correlated to productivity growth, acquiring ICTs is not enough for countries to derive economic benefits (OECD 2003). This is taken into account when thinking of the proper strategies that will lead towards the information society. Different initiatives have taken place from the EU to help countries and regions building national and regional ICT strategies. ICT adoption and its impact in economy and society has been especially vigorous in certain Member States (e.g., Ireland, Finland), while this effect has still not materialized in most EU countries (Van Ark and Inklaar 2005). From the policy point of view, the concept of information and knowledge societies, raise the awareness of the need to adopt regional policies together with country level initiatives, since the impact is visible.

The key documents that set forth the assumptions and guidelines for the construction of the information society include (Olszak et al. 2009):

- *e*Europa 2002—An Information Society for All. This initiative aimed to accelerate the actions towards the transformation of the European society into the global information society. The program assumptions of *e*Europa were to stimulate the growth in employment, work efficiency, competitiveness of European products in the world's markets, and positively affect the European social and economic life as such.
- *e*Content—a long-term EU program, aimed at stimulating the development and implementing the European digital resources in the global networks as well as promoting the linguistic variety in the information society.
- *e*Europa + 2003 et seq.—A Co-operative Effort to Implement the Information Society in Europe.
- An action plan produced by candidate countries, supported by the European Commission, and similar to the action plan of *e*Europa 2002.

It should be noticed that the program for the construction of the European regional structure of the information society is based on three basic theses:

- The economic transformation of regions based on knowledge and technological innovativeness
- e-Europe Region, which is the information society for the regional development, and protection of the regional identity and the sustainable development ("Information Society…," 2000; "The Regions…," 2001). This program has laid the foundations for the determination of the national policy aimed at the development of the regional structure of the information society. It focuses, first of all, on:
  - Increasing the awareness of inhabitants and businesses in the region in terms of ICT applications
  - Carrying out the social exclusion prevention policy
  - Strengthening the region's competitiveness and attractiveness
  - Taking measures in order to improve labor market training and intensify actions related to education and innovativeness, including

    Efforts aimed at the development of the information society into investment Plans and structural changes in regions
    Promoting regional initiative of the information society, including pilot projects.

Some consider the extent of ICT adoption a prime factor in the rapid development of countries. A study claims that ICT diffusion accounts for up to 90 % of the increase in the Human Development Index (HDI) observed in some nations. It is clear that ICTs have an important role to play in fighting poverty and in achieving the MDGs. For this reason, many international organizations have paid close attention to the strategic needs of counties in this regard. In 2000, when G-8 countries developed a vision of the emerging information society—the Okinawa Charter on Global Information Society—they proposed the priorities for developing countries as well. And to chart the way forward for these countries, they established a Digital Opportunities Task Force, more commonly known as the DOT Force (Gurumurthy and Singh 2005). ICTs can have a dramatic impact on achieving specific social and economic development goals as well as play a key role in broader national development strategies (Digital Opportunity Initiative 2001).

The DOT Force report[3] recommended that national e-strategies "should commit, in particular, to the establishment of an enabling, pro-competitive regulatory and policy framework as well as the associated institutional policy-making and regulatory capacity, including self-regulatory mechanisms…." The report also observed that "… access to, and effective use of the tools and networks of the new global economy, and the innovations they make possible, are critical to poverty reduction, increased social inclusion and the creation of a better life for all."

1.1   National ICT Strategies, Vision, and Priorities

As countries and jurisdictions position themselves to take better advantage of ICTs, they need to reflect on their response to the rapid transformations brought about by the information economy. One possible starting point is an exercise to help focus on the long-term implications of the diffusion of ICTs. An outcome of this effort could be a vision statement outlining a short- to long-term scenario for ICT development, including measurable outcomes or benchmarks over a given time frame.

A vision statement could be written for an organization, a community, or even a household. It could even incorporate personal goals. Vision statements can and probably should include quantitative results such as the number of computers per user, the bandwidth available on a per capita basis, the number of devices that will be available, and the percentage of Gross Domestic Product (GDP) that can be assigned to the introduction and deployment of ICTs. With quantitative results or measurable outcomes, comparative analysis and benchmarking are possible.

In visioning and in developing ICT strategies, it is important to think strategically of ICTs as enablers of human development. It is imperative to consider how enhanced access to information can improve the lives of people as well as stimulate the economy and streamline government. In thinking strategically of the role of ICTs and information in development, the first thing to do is to identify the development priorities and challenges facing the country. With a description of the current development situation, it is possible to consider the extent to which greater access to information and ICTs can contribute to bettering people's lives.

---

[3] *Digital Opportunities for All* : *Meeting the Challenge* (http://www.itu.int/wsis/docs/background/general/reports/26092001_dotforce.htm)

The information society, as expressed by many authors, must be firstly the filed where private sector will provide the necessary infrastructure, product and services and will impact with its performance, while it must be supported by the public sector which must provide "enabling conditions" for private sector activities. This support has mostly consisted in developed countries in providing the necessary regulatory framework, strategies and plans. In fact public sector is not involved in constructing basic infrastructures or other investments and responsibilities.

Anyway, there are differences in this approach between countries. According to neoliberals, it's the techno-economic rationality that leads the direction of socioeconomic change as a result of new technology. This has resulted in growth of the countries, which economies are more developed from the technological perspective. In order to effectively implement this rationality, policies and strategies for ICT and socioeconomic change, countries should consider the specific organizational or national, social, cognitive, technological, and economic context. It is clear that the socioeconomic conditions in developing countries affect also the context of the study of ICT in those countries, which may not fit easily with the patterns that govern ICT innovation in developed economies. Some authors stress the fundamentally different characteristics of socialeconomic structure, as the existence of the large population in rural areas and immediate needs for improved health and educational services. The ICT literature to date almost in all research highlights the development and use of ICT as a result of business requirements in industrial organizations. While in developing countries, the size of survival rural economies and the significance of noneconomic sectors show a substantially different context, in which technical analysis and the practices of IS and IT in developed countries cannot be implemented. Failure to submit ICT in contexts which are contrary to techno-economic rationality is reflected in many cases in developing countries. Thus, a defining characteristic of this research is to understand the contexts that confront ICT and information systems development in developing countries in terms of their political, cultural, and economic conditions.

However, at World Summit on the Information Society the discussions on the dominant conception of information society infrastructure, as primarily a private sector, were strongly challenged. Most developing country delegates advocated that their private sector could not provide the necessary products and services in the field of technology, such as universal connectivity or affordable software and hardware, for most of their population in these countries. Public funding for the most important infrastructures for information society development was seen as a solution to this situation. Their appeal was echoed by civil society actors who developed arguments on funding ICTD on a public good principle. Even if the WSIS outcomes do not reflect these impassioned arguments in any major way, the text of the outcome documents, in stressing the role of public financing of ICT infrastructure at many places, does testify to these contestations.[4]

---

[4]See Willie Curie's report on debates on financing at WSIS—the role of civil society, and the relevant text in the outcome documents stressing the role of public finance at http://www.apc.org/english/news/index.shtml?x=31483

As a result of these discussions, in our study framework we will include the necessary analyses on the focus that the strategy for information society should have. Should the public investment have the major importance, or should the private sector make the difference in developing information society in Albania.

A major issue in this regard is the investment in infrastructure and services. The ICT development, on the other hand requires preparation, not only in the form of investment in network infrastructure, but also skills and regulatory frameworks.

While all ICT for development documents recognize that universal access to connectivity infrastructure is the very foundation of ICT-enabled development processes, one of the type of companies that offer such support in infrastructure are the telecom services. In developing countries, it is very important to see what is the effect that telecom services under the World Trade Organization (WTO) are bringing to the regime on curtailing policy independence in taking large-scale public efforts in setting up telecom infrastructure that meets the needs of all people and stimulates structural and institutional changes towards a development-oriented IS.

All these developments have incited different world institutions in pursuing and examining the development of information and communications technology (ICT) in different world economies, and evaluated and ranked their relative digital progress. They have measured not only the availability and adoption of ICT (or "connectivity") in different countries, but also development of the social, cultural, and economic building blocks necessary for its effective use. The last attempting is to gauge the extent to which ICT and selected ICT-enabled services are being used, given that it is the use of technology which ultimately contributes to the overall economic progress of a country.[5]

The notion of preparation lent itself to the term "e-readiness." Since these developments, every month over 40 million more people become mobile-phone users, for example, and the phones themselves are increasingly powerful data devices. The Internet—now a ubiquitous platform for commerce, entertainment, and communication—has generated a thriving industry. Global monthly Internet traffic in 2010 is two-thirds higher than one year ago, according to Cisco, a network equipment provider. The capacity of the world's international optical fiber cables—which carry all this traffic—doubles every 18 months, based on estimates by Telegraphy, a telecommunications research firm. This demand is being driven by increasingly sophisticated usage of Internet-enabled services: video accounts for more than 50 % of global Internet traffic today, and the data generated by Facebook, a social networking site, is estimated to surpass that of all the world's e-mail (EIU 2010).

EIU also states that the challenges ahead for countries will be in learning how to extract the maximum economic and other benefits from the use of digital technology. The implementation of national ICT strategy and the efforts to build the information society, in order to benefit from using ICT effectively in sectors of strategic importance to the economy, lead to the need to pursue these efforts through quantitative and qualitative indicators (Kordha 2010). One way to assess the strategy and progress of efforts to build the information society is the evaluation of the concept

---

[5] See the Global Information Technology Report 2012

of electronic readiness, or e-readiness, which shows the extent to which a given society, social group or organization is aware, customized, and prepared to use new information technologies and communication.

1.2 e-Readiness, the Role of Infrastructure, and Services

e-Readiness was generally defined as the extent of readiness in access to network infrastructures and technologies. It can also be seen as the degree to which a society is prepared to participate in the digital economy with the underlying concept that the digital economy can help to build a better society. Regardless of a country's level of development, e-readiness is assessed by determining the relative standing of its society and its economy in the areas that are most critical for its participation to the networked world. So, the term e-readiness is used here to denote the degree to which a given society, social group, or organization is aware of has adjusted to and is prepared to use the new information and communication technologies. It is important to assess it in terms of defining and implementing of national development strategy. The aim is to develop awareness of the challenges and comparative advantages and deficits and to encourage development of the capacity to tackle them and to exploit the new possibilities.

However, **e-readiness can be a relative concept and it could be defined differently depending on each country's priorities and perspective**. In most countries including developing countries, it goes beyond this generic definition to include various other factors. This evolves from the importance given to basic infrastructures in the 1980s and 1990s to more emphasis on the socioeconomic dimensions of technologies today. Societies at large are increasingly empowered in decision-making processes and such achievements may not have been achieved without timely introduction and use of such technologies (Avgerou and Walsham 2008).

e-Readiness is about readiness in human capacities, political leadership, institutional frameworks, supportive policies, complementary regulations, business environment, investment opportunities, and public–private partnerships in technologies. A review of recent experiences in the developing world shows that, the countries which are the most successful in creating a favorable climate for the use of ICTs are those that make it a priority. Their determination to participate in the digital world is reflected by rapidly focused actions supported by superior planning and sustained by dynamic public–private partnerships. All these factors play their own corresponding roles in all countries, even in different ways. The underlying concepts on the above issues are the mutually complementary issues of e-economy and e-society.

It can be argued that, with their adequate resources and advanced technology, the Western countries have an easier way of implementing ICT projects than developing countries. Most developing countries are characterized by limited computer applications in the public sector, inadequate infrastructure, and shortage of skilled manpower (Odedra 1993).

Since IT became commercial in the early 1990s, it has diffused rapidly in developed countries but generally slowly in developing ones. This led to a widening IT gap, the so-called *digital divide* between the two groups. The IT gap among developing countries is also increasing.

To overcome these problems, governments of developing countries are focusing their efforts in planning and implementing national ICT strategies to build the information society, in order to benefit from using ICT effectively in sectors of strategic importance to the economy. The ICT development, on the other hand, requires preparation, largely in the form of investment in network infrastructure, skills, and regulatory frameworks. The notion of preparation lent itself to the term "e-readiness." It shows the extent to which a given society, social group, or organization is aware, customized, and prepared to use new information and communication technologies. e-Readiness was generally defined as the extent of readiness in access to network infrastructures and technologies. It can also be seen as the degree to which a society is prepared to participate in the digital economy with the underlying concept that the digital economy can help to build a better society.

ICT implementation success affects ICT facilities quality and information system quality (Westrup 2002). In turn, ICT facilities quality and information systems quality affect the perceived benefits. **An ICT project implementation can only be perceived to have succeeded if the perceived benefits are realized. ICT facilities quality can be assessed after careful evaluation of the infrastructure to determine technical functionality**.

From this perspective, **the basic infrastructure as well as the related services is object of the first assessments of the e-readiness in different countries**. Another reason is that receiving information requires information producers (e.g., data services and consulting), information disseminators, physical infrastructures to convey information, equipment (e.g., PCs and monitors) to display it, literacy of recipients to read/understand it, and ultimate application of the information to productive activities (Lihtenberg 1995).

Another concept related to e-readiness, mentioned, and analyzed in different studies is that of digital divide. Countries have been classified by the United Nations according to their Computer Industry Development Potential (CIPD) as advanced or less developed Mgaya (1999). Cayla et al. (2005) defined digital divide as the unequal access to ICT. Peters (2003) explained that the digital divide between countries is usually measured in terms of the number of telephones, computers, and Internet users. In a study conducted by Chinn and Fairlie (2001) to identify the determinants of cross-country disparities in personal computer and Internet penetration, the results suggested that the income level of different economies accounts mainly for the global digital divide. It was also highlighted that public investment in human capital, telecommunications infrastructure, and the regulatory infrastructure can mitigate the gap in PC and Internet use in different economies

So the physical infrastructure of information systems is one of the important components of the information society. Over the last 5 years, the developing countries governments have implemented some capital investment towards set up and installation of ICT infrastructure. The revolution in IT has itself been brought forth by a company of innovations in telecommunications and informatics, made possible by cheaper new lightweight materials (e.g., optical fibers) transmitting information faster. Information flows faster and less expensively throughout the globe, but it will take substantial time to reach full digitalization given the youth of IT.

Beyond "e-readiness," **one may look for** "e-efficiency," **which is the use of ICTs to reach more quickly the development goals specific to a country**. A review of recent experiences in the developing world shows that the countries which are the most successful in creating a favorable climate for the use of ICTs are those that make it a priority. Their determination to participate in the digital world is reflected by rapidly focused actions supported by superior planning and sustained by dynamic public–private partnerships. To progress towards their goal, these countries rely on a strategic framework that assists in setting up their priorities and maintaining impetus. This shows once again the importance of setting the right goals and strategy in building the information society and a positive relationship between these elements.

There have been numerous attempts to devise e-readiness assessment methods. These approaches are important and indeed useful to evaluate the stage of preparedness of a country, but they generally do not prescribe a clear course of action for the development of a national action plan. An e-readiness assessment does not stand as a goal in itself: it has to lead to the development of a strategy and the preparation of an Action Plan that will address the opportunities and constraints identified in the readiness assessment to further the objectives of the country in the area of Information and Communication Technologies (ICTs).

Although there is often pressing urgency to act rapidly, **comprehensive action cannot be rushed**, particularly when there are large amounts of funding involved and this is the case when attention is given to infrastructure. The complete e-readiness process comprises three main phases, usually undertaken sequentially:

- **Phase I** is the **assessment**,
- **Phase II** is the **development of a strategy** and the **preparation of an action plan**, and
- **Phase III** is the **implementation** of the action plan.

When the purpose is to work at the level of a country, there is little advantage in acting upon the three phases simultaneously—e.g., starting a project in one area while conducting an assessment in another.

The e-readiness process should therefore be seen as a linear one, each phase building on the results of the previous one. It is however not a finite process: evaluation accompanies implementation and with new data emerging, strategies, action plans, and projects can be improved or even modified to adjust to new conditions. Evaluation should be seen as an extension of assessment—a dynamic and evolving assessment.

Bridges.org (2005b) found that conducting e-readiness assessments within countries is extremely worthwhile as the process can facilitate and fuel concrete planning and can therefore foster positive changes for the country. Even if this process is not set into motion immediately, it can be useful in providing networking opportunities for relevant experts and institutions, thus starting essential dialogue.

The **strategic framework** varies from country to country. It is however possible to define a general approach to e-readiness: there are five main areas of activities that contribute to the overall e-Readiness of a country.

The ultimate objective of the e-readiness process is to identify how the ICTs and the participation to the digital economy can help a government to reach more expeditiously its objectives in terms of economic and social progress and growth.

e-Readiness assessments can therefore be seen to serve as a useful starting point for developing countries. The assessments provide a firm base upon which to build a planning process, which in itself is an integral step in making sound policy and investment decisions (CID 2006).

By pinpointing the opportunities for action in the five main strategic areas and by defining the capacities that can help take advantage of these opportunities, it is possible to deliver an action plan closely related to the specific reality of a country.

For developing countries, an e-readiness assessment can help establish basic benchmarks for regional comparison by market verticals and for national planning.

There are numerous existing e-readiness assessment toolkits that vary in terms of objectives, methodologies, and results. This is to say that no assessment tool is likely to cover all topics and deliver the complete set of required data.

That is, the assessment should provide examples of what has worked best as a strategy for all parties involved (governments, NGOs, and the private sector). In an attempt to provide developing countries with valuable information for their own future efforts, an assessment methodology should highlight strategies which have worked "best" (most efficient and sustainable) in attaining the diffusion of the Internet and developing the new economy. The focus on individuals, context, interests, and related activities will help all participating countries to prepare the process of readiness in the years ahead. Through information and experience sharing, the focus on best practices emphasizes not only efficiency and sustainability, but also which practices led to widespread, equitable, and development-oriented results.

The basic e-readiness framework can be divided into a number of focus areas:

1. Access and Connectivity
2. Training, Education, and Public Awareness
3. Public Administrations and Government Leadership
4. Business and Private Sector Initiatives
5. Society Developments

It is apparent by looking at the available literature that a large variety of e-readiness tools currently exist, using a range of questions, statistics, best practice benchmarking, and historical analyses (Bridges 2001). A commonly cited problem that exists with e-readiness is the fact that there are many different types of measures available today, and that there is no standardization of measures (Bridges.org 2001; Bakry 2003; Maugis et al. 2005). For solving this problem, the International Telecommunication Union (ITU) created the Digital Opportunity Index (DOI), a standard framework based on internationally agreed indicators, whose function is to benchmark those statistics considered to be the most important for measuring the information society (ITU 2005).

This e-readiness model is comprehensive in that, although infrastructure and connectivity are at the start of the e-readiness process, it clearly gives an equal importance to other factors, not linked to technology. Gathering and reporting of data are simplified by following the structure given by this framework. As mentioned in Sect. 1.1, this basic framework is to be used for the assessment, for the preparation of the national action plan and for its implementation.

Based on the information gathered by the e-readiness assessment, the **strategy develops a vision** of how the country can use the ICTs **to foster social and economic progress and growth**. The strategy categorizes and prioritizes the main areas in which to act and defines the main objectives of each action. It also sets a timeline, usually a 3–5-year period. **The strategy is a document based on reality**. Once the strategy is defined, the next task consists in preparing **the action plan**. The action plan describes with more details the various programs to be conducted. It splits the programs in possible projects, estimates budget, and proposes realization schedules.

These studies and projects need to be conducted in order to confirm on a small scale that the plan is feasible and the technological choices are compatible with the existing equipment and services.

For the five main strategic areas, the assessment report provides an idea of which opportunities exist in terms of improvement or reinforcement. It is the role of the strategic task force (comprises the coordinating committee and the specialists of the designated agency) to transform these opportunities into specific programs and activities.

This is done partly by examination of the observed opportunities within the framework of the government's priorities.

Emphasis varies from country to country and can be, for example, the alleviation of poverty, the growth of external commerce, the promotion of educational and cultural values in all sphere if the society or a more transparent government. Such various goals can all use ICTs to jumpstart or support their achievement. The strategic task force has to find out what is the best way to support the national priorities with ICTs.

The e-readiness assessment also provides all the information regarding the constraints and obstacles to a swift development of ICTs. Such constraints and obstacles are in fact an invitation to action and it is the role of the strategy to define how to overcome them.

Let us explain briefly the forces in the five categories, just to give the reader an idea about the e-readiness assessment elements and the direction that action plan must have, focusing more on the Infrastructure and Access as well as in the ICT sector.

1.2.1 Access and Connectivity Program

Access and connectivity are essential to the very existence of networks. No country can expect to reap benefits from the digital economy if its telecommunication (land, air, and sea) and Internet infrastructure are deficient. Similarly, if the infrastructure is deployed and available but only a select few can take advantage of it prohibitive costs, the situation cannot be considered as favorable for a quick penetration of ICTs, the ones really able to deliver the expected results and facilitate the eventual selection of supplier. Different technology solutions should be considered with the following criteria of evaluation: cost, adaptation to context (geography, demography), environmental conditions, scalability, and ease of maintenance.

- **Law and policies** Adaptation of regulations and issuing of favorable policies imply a good understanding of the mechanisms at stake in the telecommunications sector. Various elements require an intervention like structure of telecommunications sector, costs of services, tax on imports, foreign investment protection, national regulations agencies.
- **Community Access** Finally, simple community access solutions should be considered within this program: affordable connection to the Internet, of course, but also creation of access points which provide a way to use ICT possibilities for people without the means to equip themselves.

1.2.2 Training, Education, and Public Awareness

Lack of specialized training, low levels of education and inadequate public awareness as to the possibilities of ICTs and Internet are some of the main barriers to network development in many developing countries. To devise a program that can effectively supply the necessary workforce for implementing ICT projects as well as developing skills in the general public, one needs to develop focused projects within a long-term vision.

1.2.3 Government and Public Administration Leadership

Government leadership is often mainly responsible for network development in most developing countries. There are two reasons: first, the government has the capacity to create a favorable environment for projects that are progress related, by the reform of laws and regulations and by shaping policies and installing incentives; second, the government is generally a large employer in the country.

Projects related to the Government and Public Administration fall in three categories: Law and regulation reform and policy-making projects; Information management and Intranet projects; Extranet and e-government projects.

1.2.4 Business and Private Sector

Its initiatives are key to the fulfillment and proper deployment of networks and will become the guarantors of the pursuit of readiness objectives.

Within the context of a national e-readiness action plan, considered actions should aim at facilitating such initiatives and supporting business projects that are in line with government priorities, let it be employment, poverty reduction, or commerce growth.

E-commerce should be seen as a means of stimulating international distribution of local products, including knowledge. This has great implications in the areas of customs, logistics, and financial transactions and trade systems. Long and complicated procedures, inadequate distribution system, and outdated banking system will hinder the advantages and possibilities of global electronic exporting markets.

The national action plan should look at four large categories of projects:

- **Fiscal measures** should reflect the new realities associated with Internet and widespread use of ICTs. While the legal adjustment work is to be done under the strategic area 3 (Government leadership), there is specific fiscal support programs that can be implemented. Special programs (either under the form of subsidies or fiscal considerations) can be developed to promote job creation and business start ups in the field of ICTs and to encourage electronic commerce and trade.
- **Virtual financial transactions** are a twin to electronic commerce. Modernization of banking system may be required in some countries. Legality of virtual transactions should be acknowledged.
- **Logistics improvement** is a topic which needs to be addressed. It could imply modernization of the postal system, allowing new carriers to do business in the country and automating the customs system.
- **ICT and Internet-related business regrouping** is a great way of creating synergies and building local capacities. Projects can be done at a very concrete level like the designation of a dedicated building or perimeter or in a virtual way through a portal. **Programming and Internet and multimedia business that include design, production of content, and web-specific programming**. Also, a business portal promoting local products and services can be a great way to involve many firms not initially interested in e-commerce.

1.2.5   Society Development

Society development builds up on the result of initiatives taken in other areas but should also be promoted through specific interventions if the Internet is expected to contribute significantly to the alleviation of poverty. The projects prepared in relationship with this strategic area have a definitive social focus. While some could be classified as part of training and education program, they all give an attention to special needs and promotion of well-being. In that regards, three areas usually require most attention: health, literacy, and social and economic advancement of women.

The projects developed within the society development program are the ones that can most embody the government's priorities in terms of social progress. Imagination is the key here to use the immense leverage potential of ICTs and Internet.

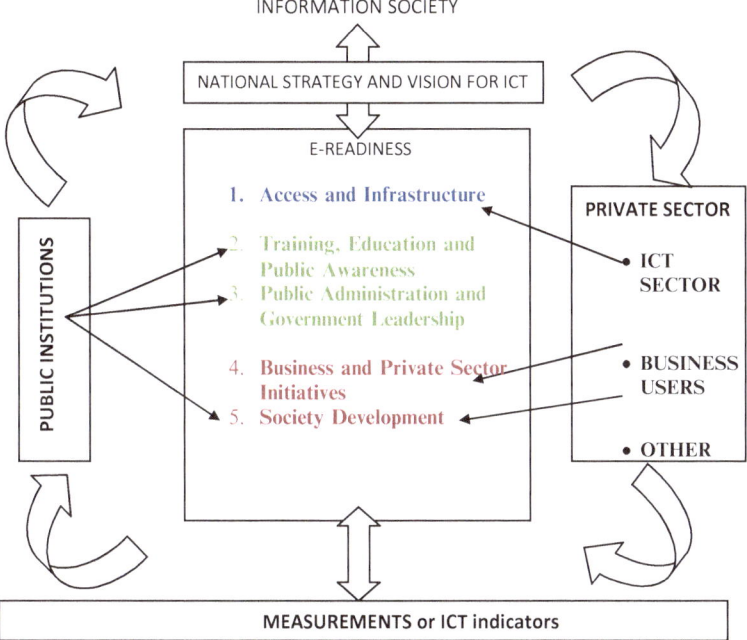

As a conclusion of the thorough discussion of all the concepts that must be taken into consideration for the building of information society, they can be summarized in the figure 0000. It is well understood that a country should begin with the priorities for building IS, through the vision and the strategy including goals and objectives as well as the courses of action according to resources and situation of the country. This strategy should in fact consider the e-readiness of the country in all five areas, listed above, to fit with the conditions in which it is undertaken. So, there is an interaction between ICT strategy for developing IS and e-readiness, in two ways. The vision and strategy should not be designed without taking into consideration the conditions for e-readiness. After strategy implementation, the impact should be seen in the five areas of e-readiness. But this impact is indirect.

After studying the orientations of different ICT strategies in different countries, we can say that the direct impact of the ICT strategy goes in two directions, public institutions and private sector. At least one of the goals of ICT strategy deals with the improvement of government services in a society, where information is a must for improving the life of citizens. The orientation of public institutions towards using ICT in offering their services, which in fact comes as a priority of government in its ICT strategy, will directly impact training, education, and public awareness in ICT, government leadership, and society development. Without action in these three areas government cannot achieve the goal of improving its services through ICT use.

Other goals and objectives deal with the private sector. On the one hand, there are necessary investments in the field of ICT, since it is a technology that requires necessary infrastructure as well as funds in research and in implementation. This leads to the private sector of ICT, a sector that includes products and services, necessary for the use of ICT from public and private sector. So every strategy need to take into consideration the direction for ICT sector, including investment opportunities, research and development, markets, etc. On the other hand, it is a sector, which products/services are required from individuals and businesses. In fact, the strategy deals with the use of ICT and business and individual users with the goal to increase and improve the use of ICT, through proper action and initiatives. The development of private ICT sector will have a direct impact on access and infrastructure, while the proper use of technology, not only the extension but also in deepness, using different functions and alternatives in all their aspects, will impact directly business and private sector initiatives and society development.

Finally, we can say that society actors related to ICT are individuals as well as public and private institutions. Their awareness and usefulness of ICT impacts directly in IS development, which we can measure through different measures of ICT.

Since the assessment and decisions about infrastructure and access are the first step towards the implementation, we can see that the last group of factors, such as the business use and society development, shows the importance of studying ICT sector in details.

1.3   Methodology and Measurement

1.3.1   Measurement of Information Society

Information society is related to knowledge-based economy; it is related to ICT usage in different aspects, ICT usage by businesses, ICT usage providing public services from the governments, ICT usage to increase participation and realize all inclusive society policies, ICT usage for innovation and increase business, etc. This is related also to a fact that ICT is a technology of a general interest, and information society itself is horizontal and complex with a great number of stakeholders and actors. The e-government of course is an important part, which has a crucial role to promote the development of information society. Measurement of information society and measurement of e-government has been in the consideration of number of organizations in international and national level. The model of e-government given below (UN report 2003), Fig. 1.1, tells us that a number of actors in different tiers, and a number of activities need to be considered.

The research on different surveys, reports done by UN, ITU, OECD, and EC tell us that the attention in measurement of information society development, and e-government at the beginning stage were focused on access and connection (Sevrani, Malolli). This is why development of ICT sector especially services is very important in the first stages of information society building.

Measurement in this sector is part of a broader frame of information society measurement, as you can see from the analyses below. The Organization for Economic Cooperation and Development (OECD) started developing statistical

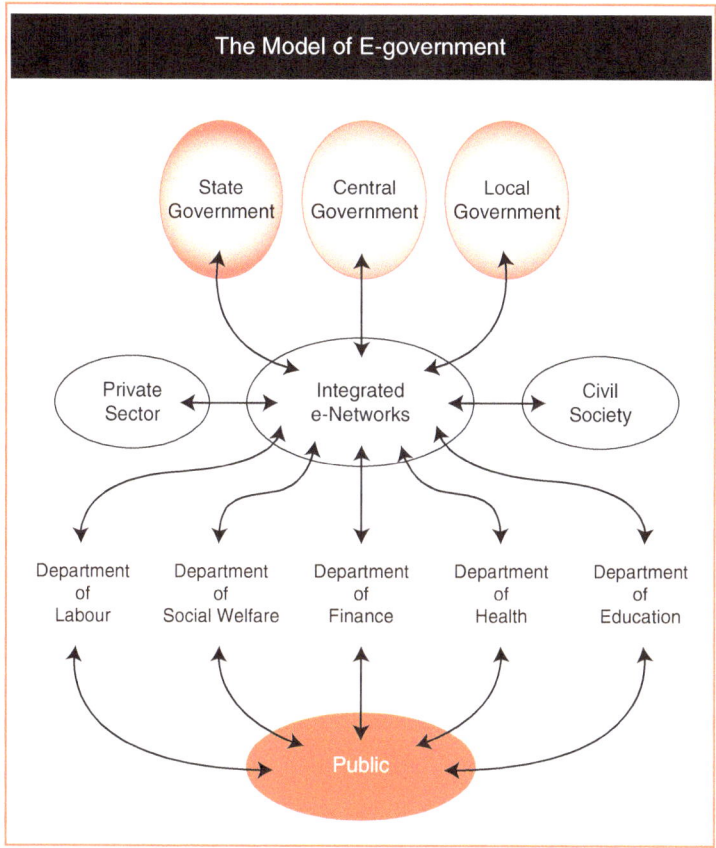

Fig. 1.1 A model for e-government

standards for information society measurement about 10 years ago, through its Working Party on Indicators for the Information Society (WPIIS). The WPIIS provides a forum for national statistical experts to share experiences and collaborate on the development of information society statistical standards.

WPIIS main achievements to date are:

- Industry-based definitions of the *ICT* sector and *content and media* sector (the most recent versions are based monistic Rev. 4)
- An ICT goods and an ICT services classification (based on the Harmonized System and CPC Ver. 2 respectively)
- Narrow and broad definitions of electronic commerce transactions
- Model surveys of ICT use by businesses and households/individuals.

A classification for all information economy products, based on CPC Ver. 2, is almost completed. It will include updates to the ICT goods and services classifications and a new classification for content and media products. Eurostat has also been active in the area of developing standards for information society measurement, mainly through its community surveys on ICT use by households/individuals and businesses. The surveys have been running since the early 2000s and use harmonized questionnaires provided to member states to use in their national surveys. Other members of the *Partnership* have also been involved in developing statistical standards for measuring the information society. In particular, the International Telecommunication Union has been actively developing standards for measuring infrastructure and access indicators for a number of years. ITU's reference for this work is *Telecommunication Indicators Handbook*, which includes definitions for all their telecommunication/ICT indicators (ITU 2007).

The WPIIS has produced a conceptual model for information society measurement which includes:

- **ICT supply (the ICT sector)**
- ICT products, production, and trade
- **ICT infrastructure**
- ICT demand by businesses, households, individuals, and other entities such as government organizations
- The content and media sector and its products
- The impacts of ICT on society, the economy, and the environment
- The impacts of various factors, such as policy decisions, on elements of the information society

For the purpose of this study, we must keep in mind an important distinction when considering ICT indicators. It is the one between access, usage, and impact. Access indicators measure what people or businesses have in terms of ICTs or how many exist in a country. Usage indicators measure how and for what ICTs are being used by households, individuals, businesses, or governments. Impact indicators capture the impact of access and usage on economic growth, employment creation, improvement in public service delivery on a macro level; and company performance, household poverty levels and social inclusion on a micro level, to give just a few examples. Impact indicators are usually derived from the analysis of primary or secondary data.

This is the level at which ICT indicators link to sustainable development. In fact these indicators are not appropriate for our study, since the overall goal of this work is to focus only on the ICT sector development as part of its impact on information society and its measurement.

The impact of this sector to the economy or sustainable development is considered as another issue, not included in this work. A distinction that can be made between indicators is that of access and usage indicators, which are useful to measure sustainable development, but they are more useful to measure the ICT sector, especially the access indicators.

Another distinction can be made between demand- and supply-side indicators. Demand-side indicators are based on information collected from users of ICTs and supply-side indicators on information from service providers. Mobile subscribers per 100 inhabitants can, for example, be computed using data from household surveys (demand side) or by adding subscribers of all operators of a county and divid-

Table 1.1   ICT indicators according density and use

Infodensity	Network	Main telephone lines per 100 inhabitants
		Mobile subscribers per 100 inhabitants
		International Internet bandwidth
	Skills	Adult literacy rates
		Gross enrolment rates (primary, secondary, tertiary)
Info-use	Uptake	Internet users per 100 inhabitants
		Proportion of households with a TV/computer
		Computers per 100 inhabitants
	Intensity	Total broadband Internet subscribers
		International outgoing telephone traffic per capita

Table 1.2   ICT indicators according access, skills and usage

	Indicator	Demand side	Supply side
Access	Mobile penetration	Mobile subscribers per 100 Inhabitants, as determined by household surveys	Mobile subscribers per 100 inhabitants: Sum of all subscribers of all operators divided by population
Usage	Mobile phone usage	Average money spent on mobile phone usage proportional to disposable income	Total call minutes billed by operators
Impact	ICT investment and economic growth	Magnitude and significance of coefficient for ICT investment and ICT expenditure on profit, sales, and labor productivity using firm-level data	Strength and lead and lag of link between ICT investment and GDP using Granger causality[6]

ing the sum by the total population of that country (supply side). Since we will use secondary data from different sources, we will have the opportunity to rely on both sides. The Table 1.1, summarizes these indicators.

One can similarly talk about macro and micro indicators. Macro indicators could be ratios of macroeconomic variables like total factor productivity, GDP, and Investment. ICT investment divided by total investment in a country could be such a macro indicator. An equivalent micro indicator would be the average ratio of ICT investments to total investment at firm level. Here, for some of the statistics we will rely only on statistics gathered in a macro level, since we are studying especially the ICT sector.

While these distinctions may seem simple and obvious, combining them into useful indexes or models that reflect the overall state of ICT development is a challenging task. A good example for this is the way the International Telecommunications Union (ITU) is measuring the information society. Its ICT Opportunity Index (ITU 2007) is based on ten indicators and uses the conceptual framework of George Sciadas's (2005) Infostate Model. It distinguishes between Infodensity and Info-use as can be shown in Table 1.2. In the initial model, Infodensity is the sum of all ICT

---

[6] Clive Granger argued that causality in economics could be reflected by measuring the ability of predicting the future values of a time series using past values of another time series

stocks (capital and labor); Info-use the consumption flows of ICTs for a certain period; and the Info-state, the aggregation of Infodensity and Info-Use. ITU's subscriber and usage indicators provide impartial insights into the growth of certain ICTs and their development across regions.

Another important indicator developed by ITU in 2008 and first presented in 2009 is the ICT Development Index (IDI), which is based on these, as well as several other indicators that are considered essential (and that are available) in terms of measuring ICT developments. By combining multiple indicators into a single value, the **IDI provides** a holistic picture on the state of ICT development within a country. It **allows policy makers** to put their countries' achievements into context, by benchmarking them to other countries at similar income levels, or with similar geographic, social, or regional characteristics. Through this, the IDI also helps governments set **realistic targets and track and evaluate developments** over time. The subindices on which the IDI is based further provide policy makers with the opportunity to **identify strengths and weaknesses and to adapt and develop policies accordingly**.

According to ITU (Measurement of Information society 2011), ICT development process and a country's transformation to become an information society can be depicted using the following three stage model:

1. *ICT readiness reflecting the level of infrastructure and access (Access subindex*
2. *ICT intensity reflecting ICT use in the society (Use subindex)*
3. *ICT impact reflecting the impact/outcome of Efficient and Effective ICT (Skills subindex)*

Reaching the final stage, crucially depends on the third stage—ICT skills, but can't be absolutely done without passing through the first and second stage, as shown in Fig. 1.2.

Based on this conceptual framework, IDI is divided into three subindices. Each of this subindexes has a set of indicators on the basis of which calculated. *The first group is the access subindex and includes five infrastructure and access indicators*

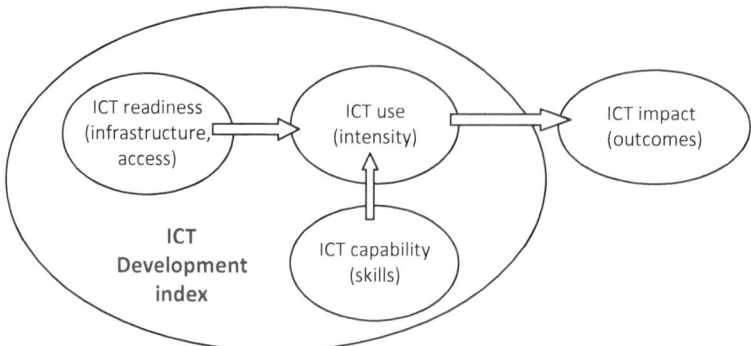

Fig. 1.2 The stages in evolution towards an information society Source ITU

(*fixed telephony*, *mobile telephony*, *Internet bandwidth*, *households with comput-ers, and households with Internet*). *All* these indicators have the same weight of 20 % in calculating of the access subindex value.

The use of subindex includes Internet users, fix broadband subscriber numbers, and mobile broadband subscriber numbers.

The third subindex, the skill subindex is compared with three indicators: adult literacy, gross secondary enrolment, and gross tertiary enrolment.

The methodology of this study includes these four steps:

1. **Gathering statistics through secondary data sources about the information society in Albania. As we stated in the introduction section**, measuring **e-readiness as well as information society is not the goal of this work. These are goals of different projects undertaken by Albanian government and other national and international interested actors in the field of ICT. We will try to focus on some of the worldwide indicators on ICTs, including IDI, just to show the state of the art of information society in Albania as well as to make a comparative analyses of the data with other countries in the regional and global level and to illustrate the importance of the ICT sector growth for information society**.

2. Describing the factors that, according also to literature review, affect the ICT sector development. **The description of ICT sector in Albania will help in a qualitative analyses of the forces that drive this sector in the light of infor-mation society development. This step is very important for identifying spe-cifics for Albania, as a developing country and for selecting the available and reliable** indicators to measure their impact in ICT sector growth in Albania

3. Listing the possible indicators for a quantitative analyses, we show the data gath-ered for the ICT sector growth indicators, as well as the indicators for some of the factors that have quantitative data.

4. **Focusing on the data about infrastructure and access, as well as on the data about the development of ICT sector, for the purpose of ICT sector growth analyses through secondary data**. These indicators include, on the one hand, the total revenues in ICT sector and market value of telecommunications and on the other hand, data about infrastructure (fixed telephone subscribers, mobile tel. subscribers, leased lines, etc.), e-education (number of students graduated in ICT curricula), level of financial support in business environment (level of credit in the economy).

5. Constructing a model that includes all the factors and testing the model for acceptance of variables. Dealing with ICT sector performance, total revenues and market value are considered as dependent variables, while all the others are grouped as independent variables. Secondary data are firstly used to identify the trends in these indicators. Then the linear regression is used to test the variables and to propose a model for ICT sector growth. This model should help ICT **gov-ernments to find recommendations on strategies to be followed, focusing on how the ICT sector should be managed just to be a good ground for the further development of information society in Albania**.

One of the biggest problems with implementing this model and also other statistical models is lacking data. First of all, this is due to the statistical system in Albania. While another reason is also that the ICT sector is relatively new and the institutions like Agency for Postal and Electronic Communications (AKEP) have began only lately with their system of gathering and manipulating data. On the other hand, different sources of data, such as Ministry of Transport and Telecommunications or National Institution of Statistics have different structures or formats.

From the available experiences it is clear that the strength of key indicators lies in their capability to address three fundamental issues: present a simplified, but reliable, view of society, contribute to a shared knowledge among citizens, and make politicians accountable for their actions. (Giovannini). However, key indicators can suffer from weaknesses, for example, they can provide a misleading view of certain phenomena, and, when looking at a multiplicity of indicators, it is not easy to derive a synthetic view about the overall progress of a country (normally, some indicators improve, others worsen) (Giovannini).

There are nearly 100 separate quantitative and qualitative criteria, which are scored by Economist Intelligence Unit country analysts and organized into six primary categories. The six primary categories are:

- Connectivity and technology infrastructure
- Business environment
- Social and cultural environment
- Legal environment
- Government policy and vision
- Consumer and business adoption

More recent efforts, using advanced statistical tools, have begun to tease out the relationships between the many variables involving IT. While these approaches steadily improve, they can approach, but not achieve, certainty, as they are all dependent on a vast number of critical initial conditions, so that as each analysis becomes more precise, it becomes a case unto itself. However, for pragmatic social and economic applications, some useful general rules and relationships can be, and are being developed.

For the overall purpose of this work and the implementation of the methodology, we will continue with the definition of *ICT sector and a picture of this sector driving forces.*

Chapter 2
ICT Sector and the Importance of ICT Infrastructure Management

While it is clear in their *application* that ICTs hold the greatest potential for economic and social development, many governments are actively seeking to spur domestic economic growth by nurturing the emergence of local ICT *industries*. This is hardly surprising, as the remarkable expansion of the ICT marketplace in recent years has generated millions of new jobs and billions in additional tax revenues, growth that has benefited nearly every region of the world. Many developing countries also perceive domestic ICT industry growth as an effective means to achieve related development objectives, including to attract foreign direct investment, provide a basis for technology transfer, satisfy local market demand for ICTs, and generate further growth in upstream and downstream industries (such as marketing or financial services).

> *Another argument for inciting the ICT sector development comes from the relationship that exists between the need for strategy and e-readiness assessment, a component of which is also the measurements of indicators in the ICT sector, as mentioned in the second section.*

2.1 ICT as an Industrial Sector

Determination of the industries is traditionally done by industry classification systems in each country. Given that ICT sector is highly developed these last decades, there is an increased demand for official statistics, in terms of harmonized international standards regarding the information society.

The main purpose for the classification of industries is to obtain accurate statistics as a measure of output, return rates, trade balances, employment rates, etc. It is exactly such statistics that show the development of the sector and its contribution in the information society in different economies.

© The Author(s) 2015
E. Kordha Tolica et al., *Information Society Development through ICT Market Strategies*, SpringerBriefs in Business, DOI 10.1007/978-3-319-17196-8_2

Many countries have based their efforts in gathering statistics of ICT in their definitions. Some of the different classifications are:

- NACE (Statistical Classification of Economic Activities in the European Community)
- CPC (Central Product Clasification) in the USA
- CSIC (Canadian Standard Industrial Classification)
- NAICS (North American Industry Classification System)
- ISIC (International Standard Industrial Classification)

In recent years has arisen a need for international definition of ICT sector, especially ICT services, which can be used as a communication bridge between the definitions of systems of different countries. An international accepted definition is also helpful in the reflection of different changes as a result of evolution and technology change. For this reason, OECD set up a working group which would have to study the different definitions and history of the industry.

In 1997, the ICT sector was defined according to the OECD (WPIIS) definition, first released in 1998 and revised slightly in 2002. It was revised again in 2007 (ISIC Rev. 4). The 1998 and 2002 OECD ICT sector definitions are expressed in terms of the characteristics of its products:

1. For manufacturing industries, the products (goods) of a candidate industry must fulfill the function of information processing and communication including transmission and display, **or** use electronic processing to detect, measure and/or record physical phenomena, or control a physical process.
2. For service industries, the products (services) of a candidate industry must be intended to enable the **function of information processing and communication** by electronic means.

The new (2007) definition differs from that of 2002 in two ways:

- Products which "use electronic processing to detect, measure and/or record physical phenomena, or control a physical process" are now excluded, thus narrowing the scope of the ICT sector
- Some categories are more ICT specific in ISIC Rev. 4 (partly due to WPIIS involvement) $\geq$narrower scope.

The 2007 definition of the ICT sector is "The production (goods and services) of a candidate industry must primarily be intended to fulfill or enable the function of information processing and communication by electronic means, including transmission and display."

For the services, the WPIIS 2007 proposal essentially consisted of reorganizing the outputs of the computer services and software publishing industries from this structure.

Referring to the Fig. 2.1, it is proposed that conceptually ICT sector could be seen as the group of activities that fall into the union of the Information Technology

Box 2.1: The 2007 OECD ICT Sector Definition (ISIC Rev. 4)
ICT manufacturing industries

2,610 Manufacture of electronic components and boards
2,620 Manufacture of computers and peripheral equipment
2,630 Manufacture of communication equipment
2,640 Manufacture of consumer electronics
2,680 Manufacture of magnetic and optical media

ICT service industries

4,651 Wholesale of computers, computer peripheral equipment and software
4,652 Wholesale of electronic and telecommunications equipment and parts
5,820 Software publishing
61 Telecommunications
62 Computer programming, consultancy and related activities
631 Data processing, hosting and related activities; Web portals
951 Repair of computers and communication equipment

and Telecommunications activities in the diagram below. It includes therefore the intersections between them and the Information Content activities. However, it excludes those Information Content activities which fall outside those intersections, that is, those which have no direct ICT association.

The above list of products and services is based on the harmonized system classification, proposing 4–6 figures, so that problems with the unavailability and credibility of data can be avoided. HS classification has been selected because detailed data are available for all member countries and also for its suitability with the CPC. According to the principles of this classification, the products included as ICT must:

• Fulfill the function of information processing and communication by electronic means, including transmission and presentation.
• Use electronic processing to detect measure and/or maintain physical phenomena or control physical processes.

Since the study of infrastructure and services is in focus of this study, the component of ICT services in the ICT sector should be of special importance.

As the recent downturn in corporate ICT spending has demonstrated, the scope for growth in the ICT marketplace, like every other sector of the economy, is indeed finite. Thus, it is perhaps unrealistic to think that the ICT sector will account for a substantial share of economic activity in all or even most developing nations in the foreseeable future. Nevertheless, it is clear that many developing countries are

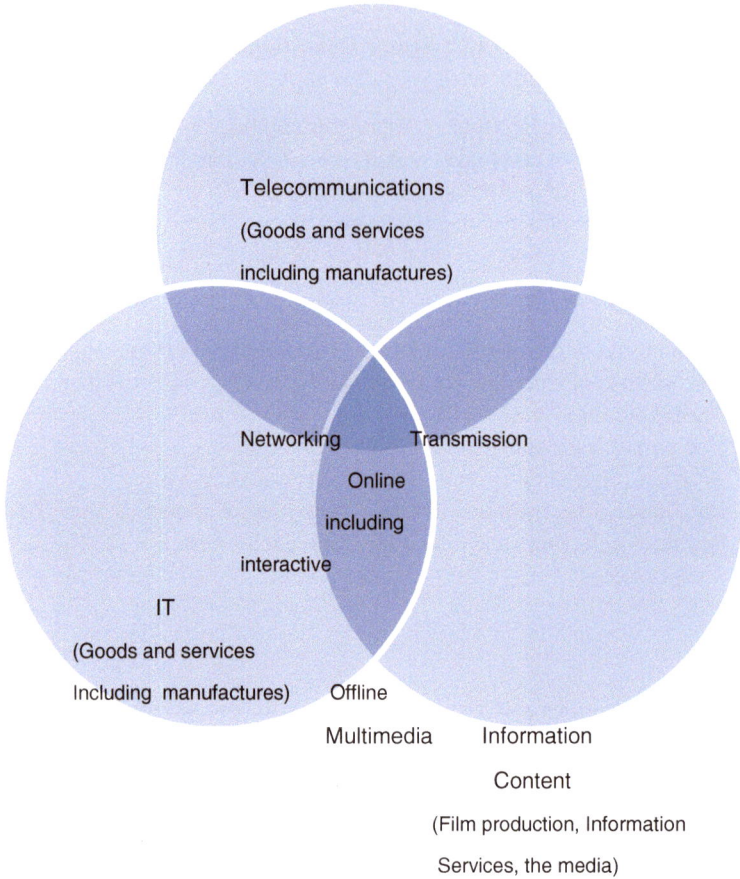

Fig. 2.1 Overlap between the information technology, telecommunications, and information content activities of firms (adapted from a Finnish model)

establishing domestic ICT firms to service domestic and even regional users. Indeed, recent data from International Data Corporation suggests that developed countries, as well as a core group of developing ones in several different regions of the world have experienced impressive ICT industry growth over the past several years. For instance:

• European ICT industry

• Combined net sales of the EU top 40 ICT sample increased by 5 % in 2010 compared to 2009, but are still 4.7 % lower than in 2007. Net sales of companies other than telecom operators increased by 9 % year-over-year, some of the growth represents a bounce back from the declines of 2009. Nevertheless, there is still a gap of 7 % compared to 2007. R&D spending of the EU top-40 companies that reported R&D spending (25 companies) 9 did not change significantly over the period. It increased by 2 % in 2010 (year-on-year), at a level very close to 2007. The European ICT industry considered as a whole came out of the crisis and the sector analysis shows that this is true for most business segments.

- The US ICT industry, however, has achieved a lot more both in terms of net sales and R&D spending over the relevant period. The main factor explaining this is the 2007–2010 innovation waves. Total net sales of the Top-25 US ICT companies increased by 18 % between 2010 and 2009 and by 22 % compared to the 2007 pre-recession level. The combined R&D spending of the same list of US companies increased by 12 % in 2010 compared to 2009 and by 14 % compared to 2007. Smartphones and electronic tablets, together with global Internet platforms, have been the main drivers of the US ICT industry growth during the 2007–2010 period.

- Russia. The Russian IT market is experiencing a strong growth. It declined in 2009, but after that is growing in all its components. Measured in euro, for the last year, the market value still remains €1.1 billion smaller in comparison to almost €14 billion reached in 2008.

- The increase of the sales in 2010 was registered in every segment of the Russian IT market. The main reason for the market recovery in 2010 was overall improvement in Russian economy and growing confidence of the consumers in their future incomes. As a result, the retail sales of personal computers, in particular of the notebooks, were quickly growing pulling the entire market up.

- Canada. Revenues in the ICT sector increased by 6.0 % in 2010, recovering from a slight decline in 2009 (−0.7 %). The 2010 growth was driven by the wholesaling industries which grew by 14.3 % and accounted for 59 % of the sector's growth. The services industries grew by 3.3 %, led by strong growth in software and computer systems design. The services sub-sector accounted for 34 % of the sector's growth while the manufacturing industries accounted for only 7 %. The manufacturing industries grew by 3.0 % in 2010 recovering from a 8.6 % decline in 2009. The 2010 growth in value added was bolstered by a 16.0 % jump in wholesaling industries GDP. The manufacturing industries also had strong growth (8.8 %) in GDP in 2010 led by the commercial and service machinery industry. GDP in the services industries only increased by 0.9 % in 2010 due to very slow growth in the communications services industries (0.5 %). However, since 2002, the services industries have driven the ICT sector by generating 72 % of the growth.

- Central and Eastern Europe. The telecommunications market in the CEE has become more mature. Telecoms are facing problems typical of saturated markets, which are lowering ARPU and higher expectations of consumers. Convergence and growing significance of data transmission services in mobile networks will continue to shape the market. The total value of the telecommunications services market in the CEE region amounted to approx. €28.3 billion in 2010, which represented an increase of 0.9 % year on year. In 2004–2008, the telecommunications services market in the CEE witnessed a compound annual growth rate of 7.5 %. The market grew relatively quickly, fuelled chiefly by the dynamic development of the Ukrainian and Romanian market. The worldwide economic crisis, together with the regulatory policy aimed at cutting mobile termination rates, negatively influenced the market value in 2009–2010.

- India, between 1995 and 2001, experienced over 10 % annual growth in the number of IT companies and over 13 % annual growth in the number of IT industry employees. India's ICT market has grown with a compound annual growth rate (CAGR) of 20.3 % to reach $24.3 billion, or nearly 2 % of the country's gross domestic product (GDP), by 2011. There have been a large diffusion of ICT orientation in India—thanks to the efforts taken by Central Government and various State Governments. According to INDIAN DATA ICT SECTOR, SHIKO AUTORET), the sheer size of the ICT market in India has a lot of upside potential. The trend of ICT market is still growing. Till about 2008 when for the first time in Indian IT history, the domestic growth in IT overtook the IT exports. The domestic IT grew by as much as 34 % as opposed to a 27 % growth in exports. India is characterized by rapid growth also in the telecom sector with a subscriber base increasing at an average of eight million per month. India is next only to China and the USA in the telecom space with over 250 million subscribers.
- Latin America. The growth of the Brazilian ICT market has been impressive. The ICT sector was one of the most affected by the economic opening process observed in Brazil in the 1990s. The relative value of the ICT market almost doubled over the decade. The growth is expected to continue in the future according to EITO (2011). The value is now equivalent to 7 % of the Brazilian GDP. The largest subsegments are telecom services (43.14 %) and IT services (17.87 %) as illustrated in Fig. 1.1. (market shares) and Table 1.2. (value). The workforce attained 392,700 employees: 26,700 in the manufacturing industry, 138,000 in the telecom services (out of which 31,100 in the fixed provision, 30,200 in the mobile, 16,100 for cable, and 56,000 in other services such as broadcasting and the Internet services), 177,400 in call centers.
- China. The ICT sector is certainly representative of the massive changes in the Chinese industry and economy. It has developed a strongly growing manufacturing arm, with large inward and outward FDI flows and export-led activities. Since China's economic reform and opening-up in 1978, China's information and communication technology (ICT) manufacturing has been growing rapidly. The ICT sector rose as a pillar of the Chinese economy. Over the last years, the Chinese government has been paying more and more attention and investing more money in the sector. The sector has seen a very rapid growth from 2000 to 2004 with growth rate of 45 % per year, from 2005 to 2007 it became a steady 20 % growth. However since 2008, it went through a sharp slowdown with a growth rate reduced to 5 % allegedly due to the lack of R&D over the last 10 years.

Although these and other developing nations have been key beneficiaries of global ICT industry growth, the paths that these nations have followed have varied tremendously. To a large extent, this divergence mirrors the diversity of the ICT industry itself, which comprises many different sectors, each with its own unique characteristics. Briefly, the characteristics of each major segment of the "information technology" component of the ICT industry are as follows:

- *Hardware*. Hardware comprises the tangible element of ICT systems. Despite the proliferation of ITC devices in recent years, the industry has been consolidating and further consolidation seems likely. Hardware firms typically engage in asset-intensive manufacturing and, accordingly, often require large up-front investments. As a result, start-up firms can find it difficult to compete against their larger, established rivals. Also, the current trend is towards commoditization of components, which may make it difficult for new firms to distinguish themselves in the marketplace on anything other than price. At present, much hardware manufacturing occurs in a handful of Asian nations, whose low labor costs and deep manufacturing know-how make them formidable competitors.

- *Software*. Software helps people use ICT devices to perform specific tasks. The software industry is extremely varied and comprises literally thousands of firms offering a wide range of products. In contrast to the hardware industry, software development has become more focused and specialized, which has led to significant industry diversification. At its core, developing software is an intellectual activity and, as such, generally requires relatively few up-front resources. Successful software firms can be found in many developing countries and range in size from one-person shops to large multinational corporations. Due to the intangible nature of software, developers typically rely on intellectual property laws to protect their products against unauthorized copying.

- *Service providers*. Service providers help organizations use their ITC systems effectively. Today's IT services industry is led by a handful of large multinational firms and thousands of smaller firms. Like the hardware industry, IT services firms often operate on small margins. As such, changes in global exchange rates and labor costs can cause rapid changes in the competitiveness of service firms that rely on export-oriented work. In addition, smaller firms may not be able to achieve the economies of scale necessary to bid competitively against large multinational firms.

- *Software-plus-services*. Many nations have developed a mixed software-plus-services industry. To a substantial degree, this pattern results from the fact that most IT service providers also develop and license software. For instance, website designers, systems integrators, e-commerce solution providers, and IT security providers, among others, typically develop specialized products as an integral part of their business. These firms typically operate with higher margins than "pure" services firms and are less impacted by economies of scale or changing labor rates. Similarly, many software firms also provide customization and consulting services to customers, either through in-house providers or through partnerships with third parties.

Depending on their circumstances, some developing countries might be in a better position to leverage their local strengths and resources to competitive advantage in one ICT sector more than others. Indeed, it is relatively unlikely that any single developing country will excel in *every* sector of the ICT industry. Accordingly, **policymakers working to drive the growth of a domestic ICT industry should carefully evaluate their country's own resources and other sources of possible**

competitive advantage against the characteristics of each ICT sector to deter-mine which areas, if any, are potential areas for long-term industrial growth.

As noted also at the very beginning, the initial enthusiasm for ICTs in the devel-opment community has been tempered in recent years by the realization that merely introducing ICTs into development projects—without also addressing other ele-ments of the development equation—will often fail to provide the development panacea that many had hoped. Accordingly, several governments and organizations have turned their efforts to seeking to understand why some applications of ICT to development succeed while others fail. These efforts have helped illuminate the pitfalls that can capsize even the best-intentioned ICT development projects.

Certain of these studies have also sought to illuminate how social, economic, and legal factors can impact ICT-based development. **These issues are of particular relevance to policymakers, as a nation's regulatory environment can have a profound impact on the incentives and disincentives that motivate investors, ICT suppliers, and users and that can often spell success or failure for an ICT-based project**.

Since ICT users and suppliers have an important voice in this aspect, let us see the different kind of policies that may be taken into account for the purpose of building the proper infrastructures from ICT suppliers or government, towards ICT users. In the next section, the question about the importance of infrastructure is answered.

2.2   Infrastructure Management, Types and Policies

Most companies today rely on ICT, which means that the core business process and the mere existence of the company depend on the normal functioning of various IT services, and IT-dependent services. In other words, the focus of most business activities is on services and service management. A successfully delivered service is a result of good organizational skills and synergy of the following three elements: people, processes, and technology.

Access to advanced information and communications technology (ICT) infra-structure is increasingly vital to the socioeconomic well-being of cities, regions, and nations in the global knowledge-based economy (Bleha 2005; Castells 1989; Sassen 2002; Wilhelm 2004). Firms, investors, skilled workers, researchers, and govern-ments rely on such infrastructure to share data and information, transact business, innovate, communicate, and work more efficiently. The availability of the so-called *smart* or *intelligent* infrastructure is used increasingly by states and communities to compete for investment and skilled workers (Blackwell et al. 1999). Citizens, mean-while, are increasingly reliant upon advanced ICT infrastructures like the Internet to carry out their daily lives, from accessing news and information and communicating with friends and relatives to working, learning, finding employment, and accessing health and other public services (Horrigan 2006; National Broadband Task Force 2001). Indeed, the accessibility and reliability of such infrastructure is assuming an importance to the knowledge-based economy and society analogous to that of the great public infrastructures and utilities of the twentieth century—electricity, highways, telephony, power grids, and water and sewage treatment—four leading some to suggest that broadband networks too ought to be owned and operated as public utilities (Geist 2005).

By and large, however, with the exception of modest public investments and programs devoted to public access and provisioning broadband to rural and remote areas (e.g., Industry Canada 2002; Industry Canada 2005), since the mid-1990s federal policy in Canada and the USA has been to leave the development of ICT infrastructure to market forces (Brown et al. 1995; Information Highway Advisory Council 1997). A growing body of evidence suggests that such a laissez-faire approach has failed to keep the USA and Canada among the leading nations in broadband and wireless deployment (Fransman 2006). While initially among the most "connected" nations in the world, North Americans are falling behind countries like Iceland, South Korea, Japan, the Netherlands, and Denmark in broadband uptake (OECD 2006). The US broadband consumers, in particular, pay among the highest prices in the OECD for broadband services that don't even begin to match the quality and speed of services available to Korean, Japanese, and European consumers (Bleha 2005). Lagging broadband infrastructure development in North America jeopardizes economic competitiveness, employment growth, technological innovation, and overall quality of life (Bleha 2005).

While broadband service is available to nearly all Canadians, barely 50 % choose to subscribe (CRTC 2006), and in the USA, only 42 % have residential high speed Internet access (Horrigan 2006). Persistent gaps in broadband access infrastructure development continue to exclude many from the benefits of new ICTs, including inhabitants of rural and remote communities, Aboriginals, the disabled, and low income families (CRACIN 2005; Middleton and Sorensen 2005; Servon 2002; Warschauer 2003). The consequences for individuals and communities without access, or without the desire, knowledge, or skills to take five advantages of access where it exists, can be serious (Servon 2002; Warschauer 2003). Collectively, the slow household uptake of broadband networks in serviced areas, and the lack of affordable service to many rural and remote communities signal the failure of free market forces alone to equip North Americans with the broadband and wireless infrastructures they need to compete and thrive in the global economy. The lack of government leadership on the broadband file has led to calls for governments to reassert themselves in this policy field through such means as regulatory reform and renewed public investment (Bleha 2005; Wilhelm 2004). A recent review of telecommunications policy in Canada (Telecommunications Policy Review Panel 2006) recommends the development of "affordable and reliable" broadband connectivity to all citizens by 2010, acknowledging that the 2004 target date for universal broadband (National Broadband Task Force 2001) was not met. Impatient with waiting for the private sector or federal government agencies to roll out adequate and affordable broadband infrastructure, municipalities and communities across North America are planning and deploying their own networks, using a range of technologies including fiber, broadband-over-power-lines, and wireless to provide citizens with Internet connectivity (American Public Power Association 2005; Feld et al. 2005; Powell and Shade forthcoming; Sandvig 2004; Schuler and Day 2004; Strover 2003). These municipal and community-based models of broadband and wireless infrastructure provision take a variety of forms, ranging from regional fiber backbones owned and/or managed by major institutional bandwidth users (utilities, hospitals, universities, and local governments, for example, the City of Fredericton's e-NovationsCom Net Inc., e-Novations 2005), public/private municipal Wi-Fi ventures such as San Francisco's (in which Google provides an advertising-supported free service), local hydroelectric utilities (e.g., Toronto Hydro Telecom) offering both wired and wireless broadband service and, lastly, all-volunteer community wireless networks (CWNs) that six install and operate free Wi-Fi "hotspots" or mesh networks in public places (Bar and Park 2006), for example, Ile sans Fil in Montreal, NYC Wireless in New York, and Champaign-Urbana Community Wireless Network (CUWiN), among many others. Wireless networking is a particularly interesting development because it provides community groups, municipalities, and individuals with a relatively simple and affordable mechanism for Internet service delivery. Using 802.11x wireless ethernet standards, commonly known as Wi-Fi (for wireless fidelity), wireless local area networks (WLANs) can be established using unlicensed spectrum to share Internet connectivity (Galperin 2005; Lehr and McKnight 2003; Mackenzie 2005; Sawhney 2003) 1 WiMax (802.16) networks use licensed spectrum to provide fixed or mobile wireless coverage over larger distances (International Telecommunication Union 2004).

Research relating to wireless networks can be divided into two basic categories: a systemic perspective and a player perspective. From a systemic perspective, research has raised questions about how future wireless networks may be structured. This debate has focused around centralization/decentralization and what possibilities may exist for network structures as wireless technology and systems become more established (Bautista and Inagaki 2005; Tapia et al. 2005). An important factor influencing these potential structures is **spectrum policy** (Buck 2002). In addition, researchers have investigated or theorized how various community, **public**, **and private players in a wireless system might work together** (Bautista and Inagaki 2005; Tapia et al. 2005). Work based on case studies has also defined various infrastructure models for wireless networks. For instance, Powell and Shade (forthcoming) name and briefly describe three models for wireless provision: hot spots, hub and spoke, and 1 Wi-Fi network also support peer-to-peer connectivity, allowing direct wireless information transfer without using the Internet. Most wireless networks are connected to the Internet, and this chapter focuses on the use of Wi-Fi for Internet access. Seven dynamic mesh. Shamp (2004) focuses on two types: Wi-Fi zones and Wi-Fi clouds. Bar and Galperin (2005) distinguish between "hot zones" and "city-wide wireless broadband," and Vos (2005) categorizes wireless projects as "regional wireless broadband networks," "citywide networks," "city hot zones," and "countrywide networks."

From a player perspective, work has concentrated on the roles that various groups may play in wireless networks. Some research has considered the community, municipal, and private sectors (Bar and Galperin 2005), but most focuses on either

municipal or community players, likely because of the **potential these two groups have to significantly alter how citizens access telecommunications services**. Key issues in municipal wireless debates center around policy issues and the legal and regulatory aspects of deploying networks (e.g., can and should municipalities compete with the private telecommunications industry?) (Gillett 2006; New Millennium Research Council 2005). There has been some discussion of the purpose of such networks (Bar and Park 2006) and the role of municipalities as service providers (Gillett et al. 2004, 2006a).

In the community wireless arena, networks have emerged from two sources. Some community wireless networks developed as extensions of existing community networks or community technology centers, using wireless technologies to expand access and coverage (Strover, Chapman, and Waters 2003). Others were established by grassroots users with the express purposes of providing community-operated, inexpensive alternatives to commercial Internet service provider offerings (Sandvig 2004), using the technology to foster a sense of community (Powell and Shade forthcoming), and/or challenging regulatory policies and practices that favor private sector interests in the provision of Internet access (Meinrath 2005). The nature of community-based wireless networks has been influenced strongly by the local context, with a variety of models serving the needs of different communities. Eight while there has been little work that relates specifically to the relationship between community and municipal wireless networks, the Austin, TX experience of converging networks offering overlapping services is becoming more common (Bautista and Inagaki 2005). In Toronto, for instance, citizens will soon have a choice between Toronto Hydro Telecom's pay-for-use municipal service, Wireless Nomad's subscription cooperative or Wireless Toronto's free community network, in addition to commercial hotspots. Following Bautista and Inagaki, we use the term "public wireless networks" to encompass both community and municipal wireless, with the assumption that these public wireless networks offer broadband Internet access. Regardless of the ownership structures of such networks, we consider wireless networks to be forms of public infrastructure that provide public benefits (Infrastructure Canada 2004).

The section below outlines the anticipated benefits of public wireless networking. Community and municipal wireless networks have been established in a climate of technological enthusiasm (Sawhney 2003), with little attention paid to date to the benefits they offer or assessing how they are being used (Strover 2003) or whether they are living up to their potential. Most press coverage of public wireless networks paints a positive picture of their deployment, but there are some examples of failed or underused networks (e.g., Belson 2006a; Ewalt 2005). As public wireless networks move into the mainstream and attract increasing numbers of users, it is important to be able to assess their performance as public infrastructure, moving beyond discussions of how the networks are built to understand how public Internet infrastructures provide value to their stakeholders.

During the past year, information and communications technologies (ICTs) continued to spread throughout the world, and more and more people have access to the Internet and its wealth of information and applications. Access to the Internet via mobile cellular networks has grown rapidly with the increasing availability of IMT-2000/3G networks and enabled devices, including mobile handsets and data cards that allow users to access the Internet over the mobile cellular network using their computers. Internet access speeds are also increasing, with fixed broadband replacing dial-up in most developed countries, accompanied by a decline in tariffs.

2.3 The Importance of Speed and Quality

Reliable, convenient, and affordable access to voice and data services continues to underpin a digital economy. In addition, as in most years previously, our research shows continued, steady improvement in broadband, mobile, and Internet connectivity levels across most countries in the world. Of the top 20 countries in the overall rankings, all but three—Taiwan, Austria (15th), and Ireland (17th)—had broadband penetration of more than 25 % at the end of 2009; and only three—South Korea, the USA (3rd), and Canada (11th)—registered mobile penetration levels of less than 100 %. More devices mean more access to the Internet, and all its productivity-enhancing benefits. Broadband is increasingly the default mode of access to the Internet: Pyramid Research, a telecoms research firm, estimates that there were over 450 m broadband subscribers in the world in 2009. There are more than 40 m smartphones in service in the USA, according to media research firm Nielsen, and more than 30 m BlackBerry devices and iPhones each globally. Even in emerging markets, broadband reaches deep—of the 390 m people online in China (56th), over 100 m have fixed broadband connections.

Technology availability by itself is not enough to ensure it can be used. For one thing, it must be affordable, and fortunately this is increasingly becoming the case. In 49 of the 70 countries in the rankings, the monthly fee charged by the main broadband provider amounted to less than 2 % of median monthly household income in 2009, according to Economist Intelligence Unit research. (This was the case in 42 of the 70 countries in our 2009 study, and only 33 countries in 2008.) Moreover, in countries with some of the world's steepest fees for broadband access, including Nigeria (61st), Vietnam (62nd), and Indonesia (65th), prices continue to decline.

The quality of access is also important. Accordingly, in 2010 we have added a new indicator to the connectivity category of our model—broadband quality. The proxy we use to assess this is the share of high-capacity fiber-optic access lines in a country's total broadband connections. Fiber networks while still more expensive than the copper networks that carry DSL traffic are becoming more cost-effective and have a much higher carrying capacity than current generations of either wireless or enhanced copper access. This speeds up transmission and provides a higher quality experience for Internet users (see Box 2.1 below). Operators are realizing the benefits of fiber as networks strain to deliver sufficient bandwidth to meet subscriber demand for video and file-sharing. Current fiber access adoption levels are still relatively low—less than 9 % of total broadband connections globally, according to

Pyramid Research—and nonexistent in many countries. But fiber is already a key part of the broadband landscape in a few countries, particularly in Asia: more than 70 % of the world's fiber-based broadband subscribers at end-2009 were in Asia, according to the same source.

Rich and densely urban Asian countries with strong ICT support from the state fare particularly well in this indicator—and partly as a result have risen significantly in the overall rankings. The fiber density of Japan, South Korea, and Taiwan is both testament to these countries' ability to execute on their digital agendas and an accurate measure of their achievements relative to their global peers. Fixed broadband networks are only one means of accessing the Internet. Mobile data is becoming an increasingly important mode of broadband access. To reflect this, we have introduced a second new indicator to our connectivity category: mobile quality, represented by the share of 3G and 4G subscriptions among a country's total mobile subscriptions. The CDMA Development Group, an industry body, estimates that 3G mobile networks worldwide serve nearly 1.2 billion users—one-quarter of the world's mobile subscriptions. Only eight of the countries in the digital economy rankings did not have operating 3G networks in 2009.

Internet users in emerging markets increasingly use smartphones as their primary form of access. Opera, a Norwegian mobile software firm, estimates that page-views in Africa's top ten mobile Internet markets (led by South Africa [40th] and Nigeria) grew almost fourfold in 2009, and that unique users and the data they consumed nearly doubled. By some measures, mobile data consumed in African markets rivals the amounts in most developed markets 2, and like their rich-nation peers, consumers are using the Internet in similar ways.

Whether used for entertainment or essential connectivity, the need for greater wireless speed is pressing, and the world's largest providers of converged services are raising the bar for the next generation of wireless data networks. Verizon, a US operator, which invested around US$17 billion in its fixed and mobile network infrastructure last year, is planning to launch 4G services in as many as 30 American cities this year. Advocates of the world's various flavors of ultra-broadband wireless technology are looking to increase penetration through co-operation efforts and standards adoption:

The WiMAX Forum, an industry body promoting the use of this fixed-wireless broadband technology, recently announced a simpler device certification process that it hopes will double WiMAX chipsets consumed globally.

2.4   Using the Available Technology Better

For policymakers, adoption of digital channels by constituents remains an elusive goal. As illustrated by the long-established leaders in our rankings, connecting the dots between the supply of services and the demand for them can be difficult. South Korea is well known for both the density of its broadband penetration and the strength of its digital vision. The country leads the world in e-government, according to the United Nations survey of member states. Yet even this country's wired citizens do not take full advantage of more than 150 service portals offered by the government. A survey conducted by the government's Board of Audit and Inspection found that although awareness of e-government portals was high, less than one-half of the citizens surveyed actually used them. Utility is the main issue: South Korean e-government channels that were popular either offered an easy solution to a requirement—such as tax filing—or provided additional benefits, such as the anti-corruption and complaint channel, which offers speed of response and anonymity. Governments should take heed: not everything needs to be digitized simply because it can.

People, whether acting as consumers or constituents, use the Internet when it is useful and provides clear benefits (see Box 2.1). Business and government alike are learning how to respond.

Google's recent entanglement in China shows clearly that this stage of the digital economy journey is different from the previous one. When the primary mission of countries was to become "e-ready," the interests of various stakeholders were aligned around a shared vision to increase digital access. But as the imperative turns from availability to greater usage, those interests can start to diverge.

For reasons of safety and security, for example, governments take an interest in how constituents use the Internet. China's interest is particularly keen, but the vigor with which it seeks to "protect" its people from dangerous online content is having a clear impact on the digital economy. One consequence has been Google's retreat from the China market. Social media and user-generated content is also being curtailed there by the government's recent move to effectively restrict Internet domain names to approved groups. But China is far from alone in trying to control its digitally enabled citizens: the Committee to Protect Journalists names China, Vietnam, Syria, Iran, and Egypt among the toughest countries to be a blogger and has recently criticized. Vietnam for shutting down political blogs.

Governments wield the greater power, but digital companies often themselves impose controls on the use of online content. For example, companies and governments generally agree on efforts to limit access to pornography (although many such initiatives are not without controversy), but some online firms also restrict access to political cartoonists and certain news outlets. The net effect on individuals' use of digital content and services is usually restrictive.

Such constraints may be one reason why usage of online services is more robust in some places than others. Only 27 of the 70 countries in our rankings boast a score for "use of Internet by consumers" (which considers online purchasing activity and the range of Internet features that individuals use) of seven or higher on a 1–10 scale. Even fewer (23 countries) score at this level when it comes to citizens' use of online public services. Clearly, there remains much work to do by companies and governments, beyond increasing physical access to ICT, to make it attractive for people to use the plethora of digital services available to them.

The next section will try to have a look at ICT sector in Albania for the purpose of exploring in greater detail how governments can promote policies to encourage private-sector development and utilization of ICTs and lay the regulatory groundwork for the successful application of ICTs to social and economic development.

Chapter 3
Information Society and ICT Sector in Albania (Secondary Data)

3.1 General Data About Albania

Albania is one of the Eastern European countries that experienced political and economic changes as the transition to a multiparty democratic system and a free market economy, in 1991. These 22 years, there have been many changes that have affected all areas of political and economic development of Albania. However, it is still classified as a developing country and grouped together with other countries of the region in a group of countries with common characteristics as related to political developments, as well as economic indicators evaluated by international institutions such as the IMF and World Bank.

During these 22 years, Albania has experienced an economic development with continuous changes, but it is to be noted that, in the recent years, has been estimated a relative positive economic situation given the crisis that most countries have experienced.

Notwithstanding global economic growth, Albania's real GDP grew by an estimated 3 % in 2011. Inflation eased significantly in the second half of the year while external imbalances increased. While the projected growth for 2012 and 2013 had some recent changes, so Albania did accomplish the projected growth of 5 and 4 % for the last 2 years. In the context of a volatile global and regional economic and financial situation and unresolved domestic vulnerabilities, the projected GDP growth appears to be realistic, especially for 2014, where the projected growth is lower than in recent years. In particular, Albania's banking sector is significantly exposed to a potential spillover in the event that financial conditions in the EU, the banking system deteriorate further. While being generally well capitalized and liquid, faces several risks which in general are appropriately identified and discussed in the program of the new government for the financial and economic stability of the country. A high and rising level of non-performing loans (NPLs) and tight lending conditions could weigh on economic growth.

© The Author(s) 2015
E. Kordha Tolica et al., *Information Society Development through ICT Market Strategies*, SpringerBriefs in Business, DOI 10.1007/978-3-319-17196-8_3

Table 3.1 Indicators of economic performance, Albania in years

Indicators of economic performance	2011–2012	2007–2008	2001
Total population (millions)	2.8	3.14	3.61
Population growth rate (annual in %)	0.28	0	1
GDP (actual in US$) (billions)	24.9	12	4.541
GDP annual growth (%)	3 %	6.00	7.9
Inflation, CPI (annual in %)	3 %	3.4 %	
Unemployment rate (%)	13.3	12.5	17
Time required to start a business (days)	5	8	52
Internet users (in % over population)	48.1	15.3	0.1

Source: 2012 Economic and Fiscal Programmes of Albania, Bosnia, and Herzegovina: EU Commission's overview and country assessments

Worsening economic conditions in the EU and specifically in Greece and Italy, Albania's main trading partners, would also adversely affect economic performance. The EFP presents a rather optimistic outlook of the external sector and does not analyze its sustainability and competitiveness.

Table 3.1 gives the most recent statistical data for Albania, according to the World Bank, IMF, and INSTAT.

Reforms aimed at improving the business climate were less far-reaching in 2011, although some progress was recorded. Building permits procedures are lengthy, access to finance remains a major obstacle to business while the program does not provide concrete plans to address the long-standing issue of property rights. Further progress is warranted in tackling impediments particularly by upgrading the physical infrastructure, especially energy and transport, strengthening human capital and improving the functioning of the labor market.

According to the EFP, credit to the private sector reached 38.6 % of GDP in September 2011—an annual increase of almost 15 %. Lending to business remains the major driver of credit growth, rising by around 20 % with the bulk going to agriculture and energy (88 %). Household credit increased at a more subdued pace of 5.3 %, well below historical values.

3.2 Albanian Strategy for ICT

If we see the economic situation in Albania, we can understand the need to embrace the development of ICT is very important and it is clearly stated in the strategy constructed by the Albanian government. It could also be helpful in fighting lower employment levels in the country and generally low performance in some sectors of the economy, which can make good conditions not only for building but also for implementing the ICT strategy.

Since Albania is fostering to be part of the European family, it is important to think of development strategies in the European context. The European development model is closely interrelated with the economic development of an information society. In October 2002, the countries of South-East Europe signed a common agenda (electronic South Eastern Europe, e-SEE) based on the European experience and the strategy of Lisbon thus realizing the possibilities for development and use of new technologies and the modernizing potential they have to offer. In the context of ICT strategy, Albanian government has included the national strategy in the e-SEE—Agenda for the development of Information society.

By joining the other countries of e-Europe in signing the e-SEE agenda in October of 2007 Albania has thus reconfirmed its commitment towards the development and creation of a knowledge-based economy. This common regional agenda was signed in the spirit of European Union information society i2010 initiative.

Those commitments do present considerable challenges, considering the current stage of development of the ICT sector in Albania. This document of strategy for ICT in Albania is dated in April 10th, 2003, document that included 14 objectives and contained several measures of priority to enable the development of ICT sector in Albania. A number of those objectives remain still unfulfilled and the development of new strategy that better addresses the demands and needs is therefore required.[1]

One of the questions raised for building the ICT national strategy is:

Should the national ICT agenda be sector driven or should it focus on broader issues and objectives, on benefits for society and the economy as a whole? Many ICT strategies adopt a sector approach to ICT implementation. The Digital Opportunities Initiative (DOI) report (EIU 2010) clearly states that while there are many types of strategies that various countries have evolved to develop ICTs, evidence suggests that an integrated approach to ICT development and deployment is most likely to yield success in human, social, and economic development over the longer term. The National Strategy for Social and Economic Development (NSSED), EU Policy and Millennium Development Goals (MDGs) all give overall guidance to the Albanian strategy. The information society is seen as one of the most important vehicles for seamless integration into the European Union in which transition from the industrial to the information society is already at an advanced stage.

The Cross cutting Strategy 2008–2013 of Albania is based on European best practices taking into account also the specific features of the Albanian society and economy. The growing use of the ICT is considered the cornerstone of creating and developing successfully the knowledge-based society. The objective of the strategy focuses in the review and coordination of the commitments related to the creation of an information-based economy and therefore to ensure a wide execution of the responsibilities from the relevant actors. The growing use of the ICTs is considered the cornerstone of the strategy towards creating and developing successfully the information society at the same time the development of ICT infrastructure is the key factor of its successful implementation.

The Government of the Republic of Albania considers the development of the information society and the use and deployment of ICT in the country as one of the highest priorities in achieving higher living standards and economic growth.

---

[1] Cross cutting strategy on Information Society, 2007–2013, National Agency of Information Society.

The goals of the National ICT Strategy are to exploit the potential of ICT in order to promote human development in the country, to support growth and sustainable development, and to increase living standards for the whole population. ICT should be used to create employment, to improve working conditions, and to motivate highly educated individuals to stay in the country. National and local needs and circumstances will be an important factor to be considered for the development of the Information Society in Albania, as stated in the literature review.

The vision for this strategy is stated clearly in the document of the crosscutting national strategy (see footnote 1):

The progress of Albania towards a knowledge-based society through a sustainable development that would lead to a society where all citizens benefit from the communications and information technologies with the aim of increasing the level of knowledge, effectiveness, and transparency in the public administration.

As we can see, the vision of Albanian strategy is based upon the principles of building an information society because the human factor is an important asset. ICT is underpinning technology for all reforms proposed by Albanian government. Albania has already implemented the strategy document for 2002–2007 and now it is referring to the improvements in the document of 2007–2013. For the period 2002–2005, the program proposed several reforms towards achieving "*sustainable economic growth and development.*" This Strategy, along with its following action plan, was build to be an essential tool towards the accomplishment of this program.

The Strategy document for 2007–2013 describes the general goals of the Strategy and defines a number of strategic actions that serve to achieve these general goals. For this purpose, the strategy is subdivided into five sections and fourteen individual goals. The sections describe the major strategic areas to be addressed and are directed to different target groups in the country. As a result, the strategic goals to be fulfilled for the achievement of this vision are:

1. Government as Promoter, Legislator and User of ICT, is directed at the government, and addresses the needs for suitable ICT institutional structures, policy definitions, and introduction of e-government services. The aim is to go beyond the first phase of electronic dissemination of information into offering electronic and interactive services. The electronic government should provide electronic access to public services for all through the portals of the local and central institutions.
2. Use of ICT for Education, Research, Health and Social Services, aims at deploying ICT for the direct benefit of citizens.
3. Building Infrastructure needed for an Open Information Society, addresses the need to deliver the infrastructure necessary for the information society.
4. Generating Economic Growth in the Private Sector, addresses the need to promote the private sector to embrace the tools of the information society.
5. Ensuring Relevance of ICT Strategy within a Regional and European Context, focuses on the need to ensure ICT policy cooperation on a supranational level.

The strategy document also includes the areas of research as well as the indicators for tracking its progress. All the individual goals cover the areas that are important for building an information society as stated previously in the literature review.

The strategy aims to develop the information society both in stimulating competitiveness and applying ICT for the benefit of the whole population. Its implementation has contributed only partly in reaching some of the objectives.

So, some measures and actions have been undertaken regarding the improvement
of the information and telecommunications technology infrastructure.

It was aimed to provide the central and local administration until 2013 as well as
citizens all over Albania with the capabilities to use broadband services. Thinking
of the public administration through broadband by the end of 2010 was considered
as a midterm goal, in this context, and is fulfilled as such. But the goal of achieving
50 % of EU average level (ITU 2011) of broadband penetration by the end of 2010
is not fulfilled.

Other measures were also:

1. The establishment of the national center for Internet exchange.
2. Offering an interactive, easily accessible way for all basic public services until
   the end of 2013. To this end, the action was focused in exploiting the broadband
   networks and access to various platforms.
3. The standardization and documentation of online offered public services will be
   accompanied with descriptions necessary to benefit from them will be available
   to be downloaded from the Internet.
4. The creation of a safe environment for the communication between public services and the exchange of classified government information.
5. The encouragement of competition among the operators in order to facilitate the
   offering of broadband services. This will enable reasonable pricing comparable
   to those in the region.
6. The creation of premises for a cheap Internet, that is, both fast and secure by
   means of:

   (a) Guaranteeing fast and low cost Internet access for all the citizens in the pub-
       lic access points, preferably with broadband, in communes and town halls.
   (b) Offering fast Internet for the students and scientific research.
   (c) Secure networks and smart cards for the development of electronic commerce.
   (d) Cooperation with the private sector for the establishment of Internet access
       points (Based on state aid or universal services fund).

Although the strategy focus has been not only in infrastructure but also in final-
izing projects in e-government and e-education, the results are still far from those
required, for a variety of reasons. The policies guiding the private sector have been
more efficient and different ICT subsectors are growing.

3.3   ICT Strategy Implementation in Albania

It is important to understand that the implementation of the Strategy should be
based on internal national capacity and resources; donor assistance, while needed to
support certain aspects of the Strategy implementation, will not lead to a

dependency for ongoing implementation. The Strategy is realizable in a time frame that is not too long, with actions that can be implemented rather quickly, over the short-, and at most medium-term, timescale, with implementation taking place during the next 8–10 years.

Implementation of ICT strategy has taken place in the past 9 years (2002–2011) and is still going to be checked for the results in the last 2 years.

Considerable progress have been made in recent years regarding e-government, creating online services that are conducive to business, reforms undertaken to improve the regulatory regime by establishing a national registration center for the registration of businesses, education by means of establishment of computer labs, computerization of services offered by customs and tax authorities. Business, citizens, and especially young people are becoming increasingly aware of the added benefits from the use of ICTs.

According to government officials in the next future, there will be an extension to this strategy where the development of information society will focus more on bettering standard of leaving.

An important part of the strategy is the definition of indicators for measuring the progress during the realization of the strategic actions will be important. Therefore, one of the goals is devoted to the definition and use of indicators that will be used to measure the status of development. This use of indicators will then also allow an international comparison of the situation of the information society in the country. A first set of indicators and the related data are included in Table 3.2

Furthermore, the strategy document has built a roadmap that is based on the strategic actions as defined in the strategy itself, which also provides a first indication of a time schedule for its realization.

According to the first goal of the strategy, one of the first projects undertaken in the field of ICT is government network GOVNET. The government network GOVNET, made possible through the support of UNDP and European Commission, is operational. Thanks to this project, the Ministries, departments of the Albanian government and two public service organizations (altogether 18 institutions) are interconnected through a high speed fiber-optic network that has enabled the use of

Table 3.2 ICT Indicators—data about Albania

Indicators—data about Albania	
Fixed line penetration	**10 %**
Mobile phone penetration	**>70 %**
Internet penetration	**15 %**
Broadband penetration	**Very low**
Number of ISPs	**30+**
Number of PCs in household	**Low**
Costly mobile phone services	
Price of Internet access	Is relatively **high**
Alb telecom	**Privatized in 2007**
GSM operators in the market	**4**

Source: AKEP (Agency for Electronic and postal communications)

the following programs: Medium-term budgetary planning, Management of human resources by the department of public administration (HRMS); Electronic system of the ministry of justice that enables court-related background check for the citizens (SEMD). All the ministries nowadays have their own websites and an electronic database that displays the laws and regulations, latest relevant activities for the ministries, strategic documents by enabling the dissemination of the information electronically, the publication of the official gazette and the legislation as well as offering an electronic service regarding court-related background check for the citizens. In the process of the computerization of the Stabilization and Association Agreement implementation performance and legislation harmonization, particular attention should be given to the continuous improvement of the information technology-related systems. This will make the "online" services regarding the integration process possible.

The efforts made so far towards the electronic dissemination of the information have had a positive impact with respect to an increased governance transparency. The government has undertaken a far-reaching reform program that aims to increase transparency, fight against corruption and accountability. The government is paying special attention to the creation of an infrastructure for an information society and especially equipping the citizens with identity cards and electronic passports. The national agency for the information society has carried out an evaluation of the existed IT infrastructure within the central administration and identified areas of improvement. So we can say that efforts made so far towards the electronic dissemination of information have had a positive impact on governance transparency and quality of information is improved. But, although progress has been made towards the information systems improvement, a number of problems and needs require further improvement: Increased awareness and knowledge across the public administration regarding the importance of the information technology in the process of information systems and good governance; improvement of the information technology infrastructure in the public administration; standard definition with the aim of increasing effectiveness at work and lower operational costs; increase of information technology capacities and human resources and their continuous upgrading of the skills.

There are several initiatives in the e-business environment.

With the support of GTZ, an information system has been established, which provides prices for agricultural products, mainly fruits and vegetables in some of the country's biggest markets such as Tirana, Korce, and Fier. The data is processed and then uploaded in the website of the ministry. This system is not digitalized and does not offer online service. The information system for 14 border crossings has been completed; the creation of updated civil registry by means of computerization of the records is in action.

One-stop shop initiative was finalized in its opening in September the 10th, 2007. Now, new businesses can register and perform all their administrative duties within 1 day and even electronically. e-Procurement initiative is under the process of becoming fully active and is regarded as a very efficient tool for the business vendors and the government itself. There is a new bill being drafted regarding the electronic signature. With reference to the e-banking initiatives, Albania still lacks behind its neighboring countries. There are several banks that apply their e-banking tools and solutions for their customers. For instance, the American Bank of Albania and Credins Bank are becoming very active in providing e-services for their customers. Customers can access their accounts through the Internet and even through their mobile phones. They can pay their utilities online using the banks' e-payment service. Other banks are willing to implement this service and have started to procure the necessary hardware. But not all customers are fully using these services. Small and medium enterprises have been trained about ICT know-how and development, basic hardware and software usage through different projects.

Other initiatives on e-busines2business, trade portals, electronic and mobile marketing, e-trade, etc. are being developed and the specific bills and laws will be formulated and approved from the government in the coming months.

However, some of project managers and business leaders stated that businesses should still be prepared and updated for the latest technological ICT developments and innovations.

3.3.1 SME ICT Training in Albania

Small and medium enterprises are considering that knowledge management should be the pillar of their ongoing business activities. ICT development is becoming the most necessary tools in terms of knowledge management for the companies. There have been a small number of training programs focused at small and medium enterprises ICT know-how and development currently operating in Albania. These training workshops and programs were focused mostly on basic hardware and software usage for micro and small companies. The trainings were on the use of Office software, basic internet software, etc. However, there is a lot more to be done on the training of more advanced ICT technologies for Albanian companies. As we firmly believe that our small and medium enterprises should be fully prepared and updated for the latest technological ICT developments and innovations. The Government of Albania is preparing to undertake some special ICT training activities in collaboration with businesses, CISCO Academy and Microsoft Training Centre. These special training courses lasted from 2009 to 2010 and they equipped and trained the local SME-s with the full technical knowledge needed.

Implementation of these projects as part of fulfilling National ICT strategy has shown also **some problems**. One of them is the ICT infrastructure expansion. Although the private sector of ICT is developing, there is still lack of ICT infrastructure especially in rural areas due to the big amount of investment needed. So, companies that are investing in ICT infrastructure as part of their business should be incentivized to improve their investment strategies.

Another area of further improvement must be the continuous training of users (businesses and individuals) to keep in touch with latest technologies. Especially, business should be incited to use more in depth ICTs with the aim of bettering their businesses. Not only spread and diffusion but also technology penetration must be considered in this regard.

Data gathered from the interviewees showed that there are some best practices within Albanian companies using ICT (Kordha et al. 2011). These cases and the gaining of competitive advantages must be emphasized in the next action plans involving businesses.

While individual users need actions involving prices and availability of services regarding ICT use and access.

3.4 Measurement of Information Society in Albania, a Comparative Analyses with SEE Countries

Even there is not yet any overall measurement of information society in Albania, development of information society or e-government in Albania has been part of the reports and studies done in global level by ITU, UN, or other regional surveys. In national level, there are some surveys done recently linked with e-government services, such as surveys done by Institute for Development Research and Alternatives (IDRA) on specific services such as e-taxes, e-procurement, or licensing center. There are also different statistical report published by AKEP (Agency for Electronic and Postal Communications), but they include mostly telecommunication indicators, access and connectivity figures. There are some presentations done by National Agency for Information Society (NAIS), on e-government development as service offered, but there is not any overall measurement done considering usage of e-services, the way or reason of their usage, etc. there are some indicators related to ICT included on the enterprises survey done by INSTAT, but not any specific survey focused only on information society. The reports studied and presented in this work, tell us that there are a great number of indicators, need to be considered, monitored, and measured.

Based on the figures, published on surveys and reports of UN and ITU we will give below the situation of Albania regarding IDI index during the years. As it was mentioned above, ITU has developed for some years IDI Index of ICT Development in order to assess the development of information society.

The following Table 3.3 provides the IDI index for Albania compared to the World IDI average over time. "According to ITU measurement of information society" Sweden ranks in the second place, with an index of 8.45 in 2012, being the

Table 3.3 IDI and subindexes, comparison of Albania with world average according the years

	2002		2007		2008		2010	
	World Avg	Albania	World Avg	Albania	World Avg	Albania	World Avg	Albania
IDI	2.48	1.92	3.4	2.73	3.6	2.99	4.08	3.61
Access subindex	2.68	1.87	3.91	2.83	4.05	3.05	4.53	3.93
Usage subindex	0.54	0.01	1.43	0.63	1.75	0.91	2.37	1.69
Skills subindex	5.95	5.82	6.31	6.69	6.49	7.04	6.58	6.83

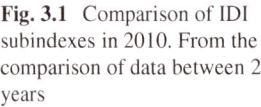

Fig. 3.1 Comparison of IDI subindexes in 2010. From the comparison of data between 2 years

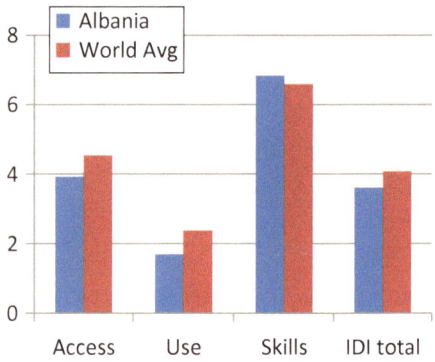

most developed country in Europe. The Republic of Korea is in the top of the list, with an index of 8.57 in 2012.

As the Table 3.3 and Fig. 3.1 show, Albania has an Access subindex lower than world average and also the Use subindex is lower, 1.69 from 2.37. The factor that affects these figures is the very low number of broadband connections and also the zero level of mobile broadband penetration. ITU has accepted in report that broadband connection considered the connection that provides the speed 256 kb/s.

But this is not the case with the Skills subindex, which is relatively higher. In fact, the overall IDI index is lower than the world average, and much lower than the Europe Average, specifically 6.42 in 2010. In the 2008 data, as well as in those of 2010, we see a better position of Albania compared to the world average regarding people skills to use the technology. This is a situation to be expected given that human resources are listed one of the strengths of Albania in strategic documents for ICT and analysis for measuring e-readiness.

Albania is developed in terms of building the information society related to ranking. Its position has moved from 81 in 2008 to 78 in 2010, but slightly lower in 2011, in the 80th position, where it remains from the data of 2012. This is not a very big difference because as we shall see in Table 3.4 there are countries which have moved more, such as Moldova. However, among the three components of the information society that have developed more, we see that in Access subindex, Albania has moved ten places up; in the Use subindex has moved five places upend in the Skills subindex it is actually 3 places lower than in 2008. We can see as well as in Fig. 3.2 that the access and Use subindexes are higher, meaning that Albania has advanced in the construction of the information society over time, also thanks to the priorities that Albanian government has set, as discussed above, but also thanks to the implementation of various projects. Improvements are made in access and use of technology, but the Skills subindex does not show the same. It is slightly lower in 2011 than in 2010, while during 2002–2008 has been rising, since the focus of activities related to ICT has been primary access and use, in the recent years.

A more useful analysis is the comparison of the indicators with the SEE countries, since their similar characteristics regarding the economy development and problems as well as the existence of the e-SEE agenda for sustainable development

Table 3.4 IDI and ranking data about SEE countries

Year	2011		2010		2008		Change in	
Country	Rank	IDI	Rank	IDI	Rank	IDI	IDI rank	IDI value in percentage
Sweden	2	8.34	2	8.23	2	7.53	0	9.296148738
Slovenia	25	6.7	24	6.75	24	6.19	0	9.046849758
Greece	33	6.14	30	6.28	30	5.7	0	10.1754386
Croatia	37	6.67	31	6.21	36	5.43	5	14.36464088
Romania	52	5.13	48	5.2	46	4.67	−2	11.3490364
Bulgaria	51	5.2	49	5.19	45	4.75	−4	9.263157895
Serbia	48	5.4	50	5.11	47	4.51	−3	13.3037694
Montenegro	51	5.13	51	5.03	50	4.29	−1	17.24941725
TFYR Maced	54	5.05	53	4.98	52	4.2	−1	18.57142857
Moldova	62	4.55	57	4.47	64	3.57	7	25.21008403
Turkey	69	4.38	59	4.42	60	3.81	1	16.01049869
BiH	63	4.53	63	4.31	63	3.58	0	20.39106145
Albania	80	3.78	78	3.61	81	2.99	3	20.73578595
Chad	154		152	0.83	151	0.8	−1	3.75

Source: ITU Information society measurement report 2011 and 2012

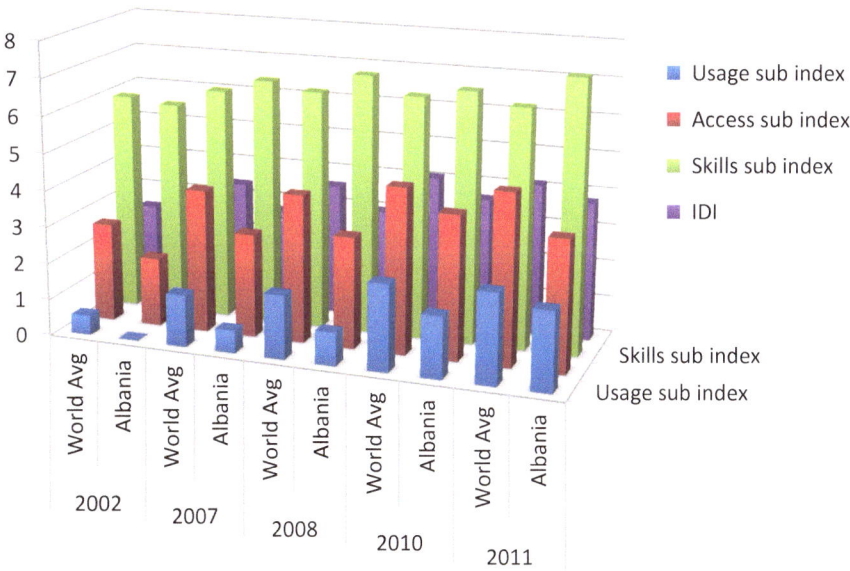

Fig. 3.2 Evolution of IDI and subindexes over time and comparison with world avg. (*Source*: ITU, Information Society measurement report, 2011–2012)

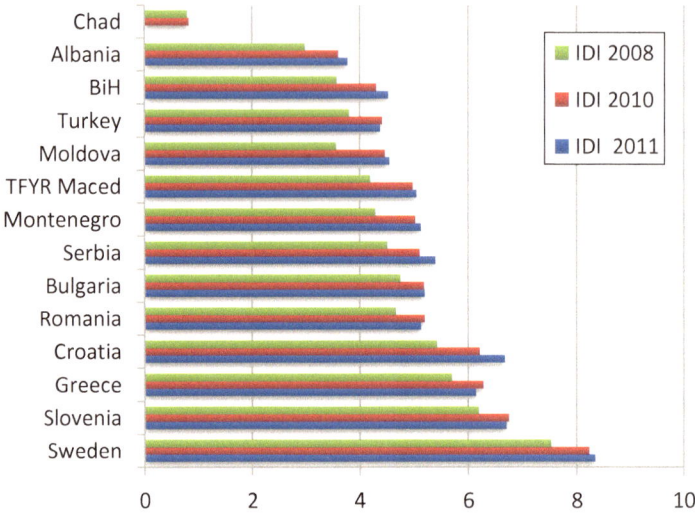

Fig. 3.3 IDI for developing countries in the SEE region

through ICT and their efforts for building Information Society. While in the data are included also Sweden, which is the European country with the highest IDI and Chad, which is the country with the lowest value of IDI out of data for 152 countries. Table 3.4 and Fig. 3.3 show that Albania remains still the last country from SEE countries according to IDI that shows a low level of information society development. According to the ITU information society measurement reports of 2012 and 2010, results that Albania is part of the group of countries with average score (result) of IDI index.

During the period 2002–2008, Albania has moved from the position of 35 in the group of "medium," in place of 15 of this group. In 2002, part of this group of countries, were 58 countries among which Macedonia, Romania, Turkey, Bosnia, Montenegro, and Serbia, which have passed in the group of countries with the over average result. To pass to the group of countries with over average level, should at least reach the minimum value of the IDI index for the "upper" group. Anyway, it should be mentioned that relative growth of IDI index is influenced not only from local result but also from developments in global level. In this process should be considered that the number of studied countries has increased from 144 in 2002 to 154 in 2007 and 159 in 2008, but decreased in 152 in 2010, and increased in 154 in 2011.[2] As we can see, Albania together with Bosnia and Herzegovina are the countries that have experienced the major changes in IDI value in the last years.

Changes that have been done in Information Society development in all SEE countries are shown in Fig. 3.4 where it can easily be seen that Moldova is the country with the highest changes in percentage, as well as in ranking, in a position of

---

[2] The last figures for years 2010–2011 are available in "Measuring Information Society Report—2012. Statistics about 2012 are not yet available.

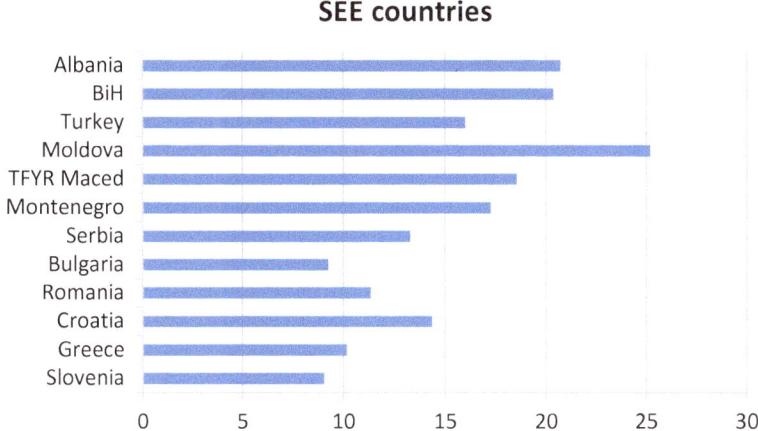

Fig. 3.4 Countries with the highest development according to IDI change

seven places higher in 2011 than in 2008. Albania in fact is one of the countries that have a level of IDI change of 20 %, along with Bosnia and Herzegovina. These facts show for a serious engagement of Albania in building information society, but still relatively low levels of development.

3.4.1   e-Readiness Measurement

The pace of change and technological evolution has accelerated greatly over the last decades, with unequivocally positive transformations for societies, companies, and individuals.[3] The society as a whole has easily adopted these innovations. ICT has provided the foundation for the changes that the world has witnessed in the last few decades. Its impact can be grouped into at least three distinct categories: economic, business, and social. The three are interrelated, in the sense that what happens in each is both cause and consequence of what happens in the others.

Another trend in the new economy and Information Society is Hyper-connectivity. Over the past decade, the world has become increasingly "hyper-connected." We live in an environment where the Internet and its associated services are accessible and immediate, where people and businesses can communicate with each other instantly, and where machines are equally interconnected with each other. The exponential growth of mobile devices, big data, and social media are all drivers of this process of hyper-connectivity. Consequently, we are beginning to see funda-mental transformations in society. Hyper-connectivity is redefining relationships

---

[3] http://www.satnac.org.za/proceedings/2011/papers/Posters/231.pdf

between individuals, consumers and enterprises, and citizens and the state. It is introducing new opportunities to increase productivity and well-being by redefining the way business is done, generating new products and services, and improving the way public services are delivered.[4] But there are also some challenges related to hyper-connectivity risks such as cybercrime, privacy, the flow of personal data, individual rights, and access to information.

As different industries change and are interrelated with each other, even more, day by day, traditional organizations and industry infrastructures are facing challenges, with results in policies and regulations. For example, in terms of security and surveillance, hyper-connectivity is transforming the way people, objects, and even animals are being monitored. Experts also predict it will have an impact on inventory, transport and fleet management, wireless payments, navigation tools, and so on. The impact of ICT on different facets of life and work is growing. In this context, the way we monitor, measure, and benchmark the deployment and impacts of ICT must evolve to take into account the rapid changes and consequences of living in a hyper-connected world.

As it was said before, there are different approaches to e-readiness assessment. Whichever approach the country adopts, it shall be implemented systematically and used consistently in time. That is the only way it can produce useful results.

In a situation when most of the world has achieved "e-readiness" to one degree or another, Albania is also trying to do its best in this regard, compared with other SEE countries. But let us learn how some of these measurements mentioned before apply in Albania to reflect ICT development.

With the exception of Croatia, actually none of the countries in the SEE region has systematic and consistent process of e-readiness assessment. There are neither governmental nor nongovernment institutions that are dedicated to long-term assessment of country's e-readiness.

The overall assessment is not very encouraging but it is hard to measure exact level of e-readiness in the region, especially changes and trends in last few years. Since the assessment of country's e-readiness is one of the most important inputs for ICT strategy formulation and implementation, these countries have to refer to existing external assessments that have only in the late years provided clear picture. So, the economist Intelligence Unit has published annual e-readiness rankings of the world's largest economies since 2000. It carries out its own assessment of e-readiness that serves as a useful tool for those developing countries included in the rankings that do not have their models for e-readiness assessments, offering them data at no cost. Most recently, the rankings of 2012 include the values for 142 countries. The methodology of this system is continuously updated so as to keep on par with the constantly changing nature of digital environment, ensuring that the rankings continually remain relevant in today's world (EIU 2005)

As a result of these changes, the last assessments of the EIU 2012 describe a comprehensive review process of the NRI framework that has been undertaken guided by a process of high-level consultations with academic experts, policymakers,

---

[4] http://sbr.com.sg/information-technology/news/singapore-asias-lone-hyperconnected-state

and representatives of the ICT industry (EIU 2012). The results of this new framework are serving for our measurement and comparative analyses between SEE
countries.

The evolved framework is inspired by five underlying principles:

1. Measuring the economic and social impacts of ICT is crucial.
2. An enabling environment determines the capacity of an economy and society to
   benefit from the use of ICT.
3. ICT readiness and usage remain key drivers and preconditions for obtaining any
   impacts.
4. All factors interact and coevolve within an ICT ecosystem.
5. The framework should provide clear policy orientations and identify public–private partnership opportunities.

Overall, Europe remains at the forefront of the efforts to leverage ICT to transform its economy and society (EIU 2012). The EIU rankings show seven European
countries in the first positions about ICT development, where the Nordic countries,
including Sweden are at the very top. But there are important distinctions within the
region. Four broadly defined groups of countries sharing different ICT development
paths and facing different challenges to further leverage ICT can be identified: the
Nordic countries, advanced economies of Western Europe, Southern Europe, and
Central and Eastern Europe (EIU 2012).

Central and Eastern Europe presents a mixed picture in terms of ICT development. While some large countries in Central Europe share similar characteristics,
others confront specific challenges that influence their capacity to take advantage of
the potential of ICT.

The Table 3.5 shows the Measurement of NRI for Albania in 2011, 2012 according to EIU, detailed in the subindexes that show the different aspects of the readiness to be part of a networked world. The figures show improvements in rankings in
all subindexes, but the most improved is the Readiness subindex, in ranking and in
values. The same can be seen clearer in Fig. 3.5 where the three values for subindexes for the years 2011, 2012 are represented graphically. The difference between
the figures in the 2 years is also the change in the NRI subindexes, where in 2012 it
is added the Impact subindex as an important aspect of the measurement for the
economies of the world.

Table 3.5 Network readiness index and subindexes for Albania in 2011, 2012		2011		2012	
	NRI	Rank	Score	Rank	Score
	Environment subindex	95	3.5	82	3.7
	Readiness subindex	89	4	65	4.78
	Usage subindex	79	3.2	62	3.66
	Impact subindex	70	3.0	72	3.4
	NRI	87	3.56	68	3.89

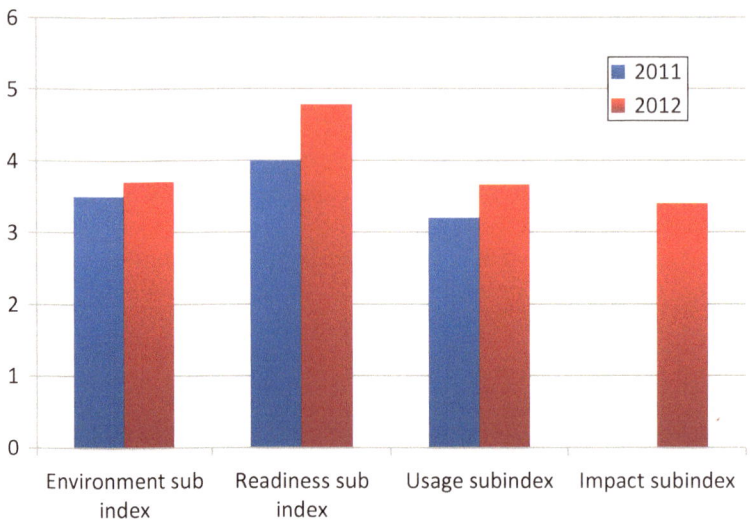

Fig. 3.5 Raise in NRI subindexes in Albania

A comparative analysis is presented in the Table 3.6. The measurements in the NRI have changed regarding also the subindexes. The Table 3.6 shows the data about NRI in 2011, respectively, the subindexes in the three categories, environment, readiness, and use, for Albania, Sweden, which is the country that remains the first in the world NRI ranking and the group of Europe and Central Asia which includes our SEE countries.

On the other hand, the Table 3.7 shows the figures for 2012, where there is a reorganization of the subindexes and the elements taken in consideration in each of them. The highest values of all the subindexes are those of skills, or individual readiness, while the lowest values that contribute to NRI score are business, usage, economic impact, and political and regulatory environment. These figures show for the readiness of Albanian Society is most related to the people skills needed to use ICTs. Individuals are in fact not only using ICTs but also benefiting from their use in their personal, social, and work environment. On the other hand, the political and regulatory environment has not done the maximum efforts for regulations especially in some of the aspects of ICT sector related to property rights, research and development, etc.

While, in comparison with the Southern Eastern Europe, Albania does better only in government usage since the services that have been entirely changed by ICTs are those offered by government, as interactive public services—public procurement, e-taxing, creation of public Internet access points in City Halls/ Communes, Designing cultural/tourism online services, etc.

Albania still remains behind in all the other elements of NRI subindexes.

Figure 3.6 on the other hand shows the evolution in NRI in Albania in the last 6 years. It shows an improvement in the values, which is good indicator of the efforts done in this time period in improving e-readiness, and in building the Information Society.

Table 3.6 NRI 2011, comparison between most developed countries and SEE countries Albania, most developed countries and SEE countries

Country /economy	Networked readiness index Rank	Score	Market environment Score	Political and regulatory environment Score	Infrastructure environment Score	Individual readiness Score	Business readiness Score	Government readiness Score	Individual usage Score	Business usage Score	Government usage Score
Albania	87	3.56	3.9	3.8	2.8	4.8	3.2	4.1	3.5	2.8	3.2
Sweden	1	5.6	5.4	6.2	6.1	5.4	5.7	5.3	6.4	4.9	4.9
Upper middle income	–	3.7	4	3.9	3.4	4.8	3.9	3.9	3.5	3	3.4
Europe and central Asia	–	3.6	3.8	3.6	3.4	4.9	3.6	3.7	3.5	2.8	3.2

Table 3.7 NRI 2012, comparison between Albania, most developed countries and SEE countries

Country/ economy	Networked readiness index		Environment subindex		Readiness subindex			Usage subindex			Impact subindex	
	Rank	Score	Political and regulatory environment Score	Business and innovation environment Score	Infrastructure and digital content Score	Affordability Score	Skills Score	Individual usage Score	Business usage Score	Government usage Score	Economic impact Score	Social Impact Score
Albania	**68**	**3.9**	**3.5**	**3.9**	**3.7**	**5.4**	**5.2**	**3.6**	**3.5**	**3.9**	3.2	3.7
Sweden	**1**	**5.94**	**5.86**	**5.15**	**6.9**	**6.38**	**6.03**	**6.33**	**6.22**	**5.21**	6.15	5.64
Upper middle income	–	**3.7**	**3.6**	**4.1**	**3.98**	**5.6**	**5.3**	**3.7**	**3.5**	**3.8**	3.2	3.7
Southern Europe	–		**4**	**4.2**	**4.9**	**5.5**	**5.1**	**4.4**	**3.9**	**4.1**	3.8	4.2

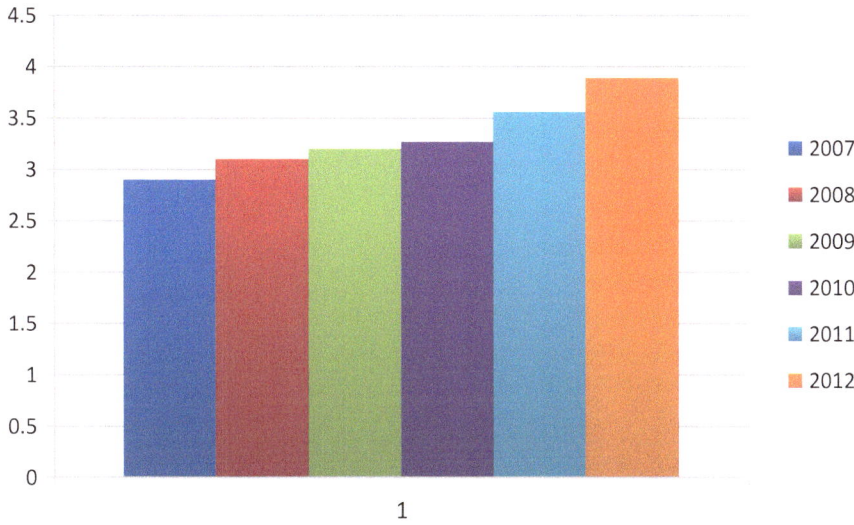

Fig. 3.6 The evolution in NRI in Albania in the last 6 years

In general, a good ICT infrastructure development coupled with fairly well-performing educational systems has resulted in good uptake rates by all agents in the region. The government vision to develop the sector and spread its effects to all areas of the economy has been significantly important in different countries. Regarding SEE countries the results show that different countries have different positions in different components of e-readiness Index (NRI). Slovenia (37th) and Croatia (45th) have developed a fairly good ICT infrastructure that, coupled with high rates of adult literacy and secondary education enrollment, allows for important penetration rates (37th and 47th, respectively). Strengthening the overall innovation system so that ICT investments can be fully integrated and yield better economic results remain an outstanding challenge, especially for Croatia. In contrast with this rather good outlook, Bosnia and Herzegovina and Serbia are relegated to 84th and 85th position, respectively, in our rankings. These scores are the result not so much of the level of infrastructure development or the skill base of their populations, but of the actual ICT uptake, especially by the business community (126th and 133rd, respectively) and the government (123rd and 115th, respectively). In addition, serious weaknesses in their innovation systems, which need to be restructured and expanded, hinder their capacity to leverage ICT for deeper economic and social impacts.

Chapter 4
A Theoretical Model for ICT-Driven Development Factors Affecting ICT Sector

Because ICTs can be applied to a tremendously diverse range of human experience, they are transforming virtually every sector of society and the economy (Riley 2000). Digital breakthroughs are creating new possibilities for improving health and nutrition, expanding knowledge, stimulating economic growth, and empowering people to participate in their communities.

Rapid innovations in technology are making ICTs both less expensive and easier to use, thereby bringing the power of ICTs within the reach of a greater number of people. These qualities make ICTs highly relevant to the developing world. As many developing nations have recognized, ICTs have the potential to spur local economic growth and to expand the reach and effectiveness of development initiatives.

There are in fact, according to different authors, some forces that stand after the ICT-driven development. This is a term that implies a society driven by the use of ICT and the development of an ICT sector. The focus here is to bring by different sources of literature, all the forces that may have an effect in the further development and growth of ICT sector, which in turn will bring along with proper strategies in the development of the information society.

It can be asserted that ICTs have positive impacts on the economic, social, and political development of a country, region, or community. While that is easy to assert, it is far from easy to quantify it in a way that yields an explanatory and predictive theoretical understanding which can be applied to information policies. Yet many international organizations and economies consider this a critical foundation for effective information policy-making.

It is not enough, to place ICTs onto the development agenda without also addressing other critical elements of the development equation. Governments, especially in the developing countries, need to understand all the forces that drive the growth of ICT sector, since they can contribute for further development. Even companies in this sector must also understand the factors that affect ICT sector growth, in order to become and remain competitive in this market. The importance of studying the elements, of which the growth of the sector depends on, is to design the proper strategies and interventions with positive effects in all the related aspects within ICT sector.

© The Author(s) 2015
E. Kordha Tolica et al., *Information Society Development through ICT Market Strategies*, SpringerBriefs in Business, DOI 10.1007/978-3-319-17196-8_4

A nation's regulatory environment in particular can have a profound impact on ICT utilization and ICT industry growth. Legal rules create a complex web of incentives and disincentives to private-sector action, some of which will impact a society's desire and the ability to develop, acquire, or utilize ICTs. Different aspects concern policymakers and companies on a range of ICT policy issues that affect users and the industry.

While a broad range of laws and policies may influence the overall bundle of incentives for ICT investment and use, in most legal regimes the most critical laws and policies arise in the following areas:

1. Policies that directly impact ICT innovation and investment
2. Policies that develop people's capacity to utilize ICTs effectively
3. Policies affecting entrepreneurship and R&D
4. Policies affecting telecommunications infrastructure and access. The following sections address each of these areas in turn.

4.1   ICT Innovation and Investment

ICT-based development is sustainable over the long term only if people have incentives to acquire and utilize ICTs, including meaningful opportunities to leverage ICTs to improve their own lives. A vast amount of ICT Products and services are in fact subject of legal rights lows. The private sector will not invest in the resources necessary to drive economic growth unless the surrounding property rules are clear, reliable, and consistently enforced (Gatautis 2008).

The private sector is most likely to invest in ICTs in an environment that provides meaningful protections for property rights (including rights in intangible property), promotes competition and trade, protects consumers, and creates incentives for firms to invest in developing innovative new products and services. The core principles of such a framework are set out below.

4.1.1   Intellectual Property Rights

Intellectual property (IP) laws provide critical incentives for ICT innovation, as they protect the work of any inventor, whether an individual, a research institution, or an enterprise, especially in ICT sector. Robust IP laws enable inventors to capture a portion of their innovation's value in the marketplace, either by practicing the innovation themselves or by licensing it to others. Intellectual property is of particular importance to the ICT sector, which is characterized by rapid innovation and high rates of investment in research and development (R&D). IP laws allow firms to recoup the R&D investments embodied in their innovative technologies, which provides the funds for future rounds of R&D and product improvement. Strong IP laws and effective enforcement are just as vital to innovation in developing countries. IP protections enable inventors and entrepreneurs in developing economies to prevent others from copying their innovations and thereby "free riding" on their R&D investments. Effective IP protection also promotes foreign direct investment and technology transfer by giving foreign firms the confidence of knowing that their investments and technologies will not be susceptible to rampant copying or compulsory licensing.

In the area of ICT, domestic SMEs are often one of the driving forces behind technology innovations. Their innovative and creative capacity, however, is not always fully exploited as many SMEs in the developing world are either not aware of applicable IP laws, perhaps more often, do not have confidence that such laws will be respected and enforced.

4.1.2   Rights in Tangible Property

While robust intellectual property rules clearly spur ICT innovation and foster foreign investment around ICTs, clear, transparent rules governing the ownership and transfer of tangible property can also substantially impact a country's development prospects. For many underserved populations, their homes and land are their most important financial asset. Ensuring that people can obtain and establish clear title to such property is vital to developing a broader financial environment that is conducive to commerce and economic growth.

In short, the private sector will not invest in the resources necessary to drive economic growth unless the surrounding property rules are clear, reliable, and consistently enforced. Indeed, clearly defined and enforced property rules are widely viewed as a necessary precondition to meaningful participation in a market economy, and the lack of such rules can create significant disincentives to foreign investment.

4.1.3   International Trade and Investment

The global reach of today's ICT marketplace means that open and nondiscriminatory trade is of paramount importance. Protectionist measures and related barriers to trade can create substantial impediments to ICT access in developing countries. Barriers to ICT trade also have longer-term adverse effects on local ICT industries because they prop up inefficient domestic firms and discourage multinational firms from pursuing local partnerships or engaging in foreign direct investment. Trade barriers also reduce competitive pressures for local ICT firms to innovate and lower their prices, which means that domestic consumers must pay higher prices for inferior goods.

Government procurement policies that extend preferences to domestic ICT suppliers likewise distort international trade. In many nations, governments are the dominant purchasers of ICT products and services, and their procurement practices can have a profound impact on the marketplace. Governments that procure ICTs based on neutral, nondiscriminatory criteria—such as performance, suitability for purpose, and overall value—force competing vendors to offer the best products at the best price, which creates a dynamic of competition that often spills over into the broader marketplace. Where, by contrast, governments procure ICTs based on the nationality of the product or supplier, or on nonperformance criteria (e.g., a software program's development or licensing model), taxpayer funds are wasted.

4.1.4   Competition

The global ICT marketplace is extremely competitive and diverse, with many opportunities for new entrants. Competition and industry diversity are two important reasons why the ICT industry is so innovative. It also helps explain why start-up ICT firms and entrepreneurs have been so successful in creating new markets and developing new business models.

The main beneficiaries of this diverse, competitive marketplace are consumers. Competition not only pushes down prices, but also spurs ICT suppliers to develop products and services that make ICTs accessible and easy-to-use for the broadest possible range of consumers. Where consumers face risks that competition and new technologies alone cannot address, governments should respond with legislation that is targeted and technology-neutral and should ensure that liability rules do not deter ICT innovation.

4.1.5   Publicly Funded Research

Government funding of scientific research can play a vital if often overlooked role in economic development. In addition to enriching a nation's intellectual life, publicly funded research can attract foreign investment and provide the raw material for further innovation and commercial development by the private sector. Such commercialization can also provide a revenue stream back to the research organization itself and strengthen information sharing between research organizations, thereby creating a financial and innovation synergy between the public and private sectors.

The degree to which publicly funded research in fact stimulates private-sector commercialization, however, depends in large part on whether the recipients of public research funds have incentives to claim title to and license such research to third parties for further development, including for commercial gain. This process also requires that research is made available under terms that will attract the private-sector resources needed to commercialize it. While many developing nations do not invest large sums in publicly funded research, governments can ensure that any such funds yield the greatest possible benefits by taking the following steps:

4.1.6   Security and Privacy

Different safety problems become substantial barriers in the development of e-services, e-trade, and other significant ICT-enabled areas (Gatautis 2008). Security threats vary in their method of attack, but collectively they undermine user trust in the Internet and e-commerce by corrupting or stealing online data. Strengthening online security requires a complementary, coordinated response by industry, government, and users. In pursuance of creating an attractive e-environment, ICT consumers require safety tools and explicit information on their usage. Maintaining user trust in the online environment is no less vital in developing countries (Chan 2004).

The explosion in Internet usage over the past decade has resulted in an increasing amount of data exchanged online or stored on Internet-connected networks. Regrettably, this phenomenon has been accompanied by a dramatic increase in the number, sophistication, and severity of criminal cyber attacks that seek to compromise this data. Viruses, worms, Trojan Horses, spyware, "phishing," and other security threats vary in their method of attack, but collectively they undermine user trust in the Internet and e-commerce by corrupting or stealing online data. Strengthening online security requires a complementary, coordinated response by industry, government, and users.

While online security threats almost always involve clearly malicious and/or criminal activity by bad actors, online privacy implicates broader social questions over the proper limits on the use of personal information. While certain uses of personal information can greatly improve the online experience and consumer welfare, users will maintain trust in online communications only if they have adequate control over the collection of their personal information and how it is used. Here too, an effective response requires coordinated and complementary action by industry and government.

Maintaining user trust in the online environment is no less vital in developing countries.

4.1.7   Technology Standards

Technology standards are increasingly relevant to development. Broad adoption of standards can promote interoperability by making it easier for ICT products and services to share and mutually use data. Interoperability, in turn, can drive down costs and expand ICT access for developing-world users by allowing them to select competing products and services from multiple vendors and combine them in a single network. Interoperability also facilitates the transfer of information among governments, development organizations, and the populations they serve.

Although ICT firms have strong commercial incentives to make their products interoperate with others, voluntary industry adoption of technology standards can reinforce these incentives by providing a common set of guidelines for data exchange. Particularly where they are developed by consensus, are publicly available, and can be implemented by anyone on reasonable and nondiscriminatory terms, technology standards can promote interoperability in a way that also encourages innovation, enhances competition, and expands consumer choice.

Although the ICT industry should always remain the principal driving force in developing technology standards, governments may also play a role. To ensure that laws involving technology standards do not inadvertently impede innovation or competition, regulatory policies in this area should be consistent with the principle of *allowing industry to lead in promoting technical interoperability*, *including by developing voluntary*, *consensus-based standards*.

4.1.8   e-Government

Governments across the globe are turning to ICTs for the same reasons that are attracting the private sector: to increase efficiency, streamline processes, and provide better services to a larger base of users. Government uptake of ICTs, however, can have important added benefits, such as increasing citizen participation and making government processes more transparent and public officials more accountable. e-Government initiatives can also play an important "leadership" role, particularly in developing countries, by providing a concrete example of how ICTs can drive productivity and economic growth.

4.2   Human Capacity Building

Investments in people are fundamental to social and economic development. Investments in technology will do little to alleviate poverty or improve the lives of underserved communities unless they are matched by efforts to build the capacity of target populations to harness the opportunities that ICTs offer. Education and skills development are critical components in helping individuals, communities, and even entire countries thrive in the global information economy, and therefore should be central elements of any development agenda. The digital divide examines the disparity in the diffusion of ICT between rural and urban, well-educated or poorly educated population (Cayla et al. 2005).

A substantial number of longitudinal studies address the interaction between technology and human capital, and their joint impact on productivity performance (Bartelsman and Doms 2000).

Education and skills development are critical components in helping individuals, communities, and even entire countries thrive in the global information economy, and therefore should be central elements of any development agenda. Certain core policies and principles that support human capacity building through education are:

4.2.1 Education and Digital Literacy

Expanding educational opportunities and digital literacy in underserved communities is critical to broadening economic opportunities and removing barriers to digital inclusion. Although certain forms of ICTs (e.g., telephones) can be and are being used effectively without widespread digital literacy, it is equally clear that digital literacy is vital to enabling users unlock the full potential of ICTs.

ICTs can also play a significant role in helping teachers expand learning opportunities. Microsoft recognizes the vital role of education in human capacity building and the contribution that ICTs can make in this area. The company supports several initiatives that focus on the specific educational needs of developing countries and has partnered with many governments and development organizations to implement these initiatives. These efforts, and the broader role of ICTs in education, are described more fully in Chap. 5 of this book.

While the developing world and the broader development community are to be commended for their efforts to improve literacy and in working with the private sector to address this problem, more needs to be done in ensuring the compulsory primary education, affordable secondary education, and more options for the university curricula.

4.2.2 ICT Skills Development

ICT skills are vital to enabling individuals and organizations to leverage the full potential of information and communication technologies. Yet in many parts of the developing world, relatively few users have the skills to utilize ICT effectively. Fewer still have the expertise to develop ICT products or provide critical IT services. A shortage of skilled ICT workers will make organizations reluctant to invest in ICT, thereby curtailing demand for domestic ICT products and services and leaving fewer opportunities for entrepreneurs and domestic ICT firms. A chronic shortage of skilled ICT workers will impair a country's competitiveness not only in the ICT sector—one of the fastest growing areas of the global economy—but in many other more traditional sectors as well.

4.3   Enterprise and Entrepreneurialism

Enterprise and entrepreneurialism. Although ICT adoption studies constitute a significant area of research within the information systems domain (Fichman 2000), there continues to be a need for better understanding of the factors that drive or inhibit the adoption and use of ICT within the specific context of business especially SMEs (Caldeira and Ward 2002; Al-Qirim 2004; Bharati and Chaudhury 2006). The private sector is and will likely always remain at the forefront of ICT innovation, investment, and use. In a competitive economy, the effective use of ICT may help efficient firms gain market share at the cost of less productive firms, raising overall productivity. Several other studies point to the role of competition. However, the evidence also suggests that these impacts occur primarily, or only, when ICT investment is accompanied by other changes and investments. Governments can leverage these private-sector forces by improving access to capital, requiring transparent accounting and investment practices, facilitating access to local and global markets, and stimulating investments in ICT and technology research and development.

As noted in the beginning of this section, government policies can have a vital impact on the utilization of ICTs to achieve social and economic development. Yet the private sector is and will likely always remain at the forefront of ICT innovation, investment, and use. Governments can leverage these private-sector forces by improving access to capital, requiring transparent accounting and investment practices, facilitating access to local and global markets, and stimulating investments in ICT and technology research and development.

4.3.1   Access to Capital

Access to capital. Several studies point to an important link between the use of ICT and the ability of a company to innovate. The role of innovation was raised by Bresnahan and Greenstein (1996), who argued that users help make investment in technologies, such as ICT, more valuable through their own experimentation and invention.

Leveraging ICTs for social and economic development also requires access to capital. For developing nations to take full advantage of ICTs and spur the growth of domestic ICT industries, it is imperative that individuals and businesses have ready access to affordable financing. Competitive, flexible capital markets make it easier for individuals and firms to purchase ICTs on credit, and make it less expensive for start-up ICT firms to obtain the funds necessary to develop, manufacture, and market new products.

4.3.2 Incentives for Private-Sector Investment

Particularly in an age of limited public resources, the private sector must remain the primary engine of ICT-based growth and industrial development. While governments cannot, of course, dictate the course of private-sector investment, it can help channel private-sector investment into pro-growth areas by providing appropriate tax and related incentives for ICT investment. Governments can also encourage foreign investment by providing a regulatory framework that increases predictability and reduces financial risk.

4.4 Infrastructure and Access

The ability of the Internet and other online networks to serve as effective communications and distribution mechanisms—in short, the ability of ICT to fulfill its potential as an "enabler" of economic growth and development—depends in substantial part on the quality and reach of the underlying telecommunications infrastructure. Users cannot achieve the full benefits of ICT unless the telecommunications infrastructure is both extensive and affordable. Governments and industry must also work together to promote affordable computing initiatives that do not undermine market incentives for innovation and product development. Braun (2004) corroborates the impact of geographic location on ICT adoption stating that being located in peripheral regions where the ICT infrastructure, especially broadband, is either inadequate or prohibitively expensive will be a major deterrent to ICT adoption.

Literature have also identified some other factors that affect also other sectors such as price level in the industry, population growth, and other macro environment indicators, but in the following section the focus will be at the indicators which will help in building the model and the empirical data that will support the model for the factors that are the most encountered in Albania.

Chapter 5
Albanian Situation Related to the Factors for ICT Development

ICT sector is growing significantly in Albania, especially Internet deployment. Situation is rapidly changing from 1 year to the other, despite the fact that this country has the lowest telecommunication in Europe. There is a general awareness about the role of ICT between people and government; and as consequence, there are many ICT-related initiatives, especially private in main urban areas. Mobile telephony has a high penetration in urban areas as an alternative solution in conditions of low penetration of fixed telephony. Despite this considerable growth of ICT deployment, there are several critical obstacles to be addressed. Some of them are related to cultural and economical conditions, for example, the problem of electrical energy shortages, especially in rural areas, high poverty and lack of telecommunications infrastructure in remote areas. A realistic view of all the possible factors mentioned above, regarding Albania, need to be analyzed, in order to fulfill the last goal of this work. It is very important to look at the conditions of Albania, in the main indicators that impact the ICT sector and infrastructures for Information Society and then to identify the areas with the greatest impact and what must be improved. So, this section will deal with four main areas:

5.1 Innovation and Investments for the Information Society

First of all, the development of the information society depends on the adoption of the relevant **necessary legislation**. The development of infrastructures for Information Society has required many countries to do some legal and regulative reforms to help with the development of their telecommunication market first of all. Countries that began this reform in the mid-1990 swung full telecommunications laws to sum all the regulatory framework. This framework is currently the most usual legislative reform in this sector. In Albania, with the emergence of law no. 8288 dated 18.02.1998, for overseeing the telecommunications sector by Regulatory Entity, as well as law no. 8618 dated 14.06.2000 for telecommunications, continuous

© The Author(s) 2015
E. Kordha Tolica et al., *Information Society Development through ICT Market Strategies*, SpringerBriefs in Business, DOI 10.1007/978-3-319-17196-8_5

improvements, and additions to the legal framework for the implementation of these laws have been done by different governments.

Since 2006 substantial changes have been made in the legislative framework concerning the progress and development of the ICT sector in Albania. These include an amendment to the Telecommunications Law, implementing legislation, and provisions on Voice over Internet Protocol (VoIP) services introduced into the law.

Nowadays, the international trend is to open telecommunication markets to competition. Until recently, most of the countries that have entered into competition have done this in stages. Competition is primarily on the periphery-enabled services that were marginal to the existing operator. The market for services in remote distance is generally open to competition before basic local services. Competition is most common in markets for new services like mobile telephony and Internet services. Creating a competitive, liberalized market and Independent Operators Licensing is one of the key strategic actions related to the ICT sector in Albania.

Some important elements of the legal framework that have been completed during these years in Albania are:

- Interconnection agreements
- Methodology for tariff regulation
- Licensing of other operators, especially for Internet service providers (ISP).

Until now, a number of other important laws for regulating ICT activities have been formulated and approved in compliance with the commitments of the SAA:

- Law no. 9880 of 25.2.2008 "on the electronic signature"
- Law no. 9887 of 10.3.2008 "on the Protection of Personal Data"
- Law no. 9643 of 20.11.2006 amended, for the public procurement that enables the electronic procurement
- Law no. 9723 of 3.5.2007 on the registration of businesses "on the national Center of registration"
- Law "on the electronic Communications in the republic of Albania," no. 9918 of 19.5.2008

    In the field of cyber crime, Albania has signed and ratified the Convention for the Cyber Crime of 2002 and has reflected in the Penal Code and Penal Procedure Code the requirements of Cybercrime Convention the improvement and completion of the legal framework in line with the best European practices is one of the priorities for the further development of the information society.

- Based mainly on EU legislation a new law on electronic communications was adopted in 2008 organizing the governance for the ICT sector. In the next couple of years, the Digital Albania Initiative was launched and a new policy paper for the electronic communications sector was approved.
- The establishment of the Electronic and Postal Communications regulatory authority (AKEP) in 2008 which replaced the previous Telecommunications Regulatory Entity was a step towards the implementation and regulation of the development of the ICT sector in Albania. This is an independent and self-financing organization accountable to the Albanian Parliament.

- In 2007, the National Agency on Information Society was also established with the goal of coordinating the development of the sector, administration of state information systems, and promotion of an information society.
- In 2008 was established also the National Authority for Electronic Certification (NAEC) with the main responsibility to supervise and to monitor the use of Electronic signature in Albania. In the same year, the Commissioner for the Protection of Personal Data was created in order to ensure the protection of personal information privacy.
- The Ministry for Innovation and Information and Communication Technologies was created in order to coordinate the reforms in the ICT sector, manage the digitalization as planned, and supervise the implementation of the Digital Albania Initiative, the National e-Strategy, the e-Government Project, and the National Plan for Radiofrequency (see footnote 3 in Chap. 1).

As it can be seen laws to ensure **competition** in the sector, as well as privacy and security and business and enterprise participation are the first to be focused in Albania, but there is still a lot to be done in the aspect of intellectual and property rights related to ICT products and services. In fact, there are also problems related to the rights to intangible property in Albania and government should do more in this aspect.

Recent **technological changes** are also changing ICT sector. Many providers transmit information over the Internet in conventional transmission networks. Broadcast mobile TV networks also are rising very fast. As networks move towards digital technologies, transmission networks may also carry a range of services such as voice telephony. This affects a lot of regulators and competition policy in the sector.

IT-related scientific research projects also are helping in the fostering of business community to invest in ICTs. During 2007, the Council of ministers approved Albania's associated member status in the program FP7. Research activities in Albania are limited, first of all due to the lack of infrastructure and insufficient financial resources. A significant number of specialists have abandoned their scientific research institutions and the majority have emigrated. IT departments have been severely affected by the "brain drain." For this very reason, public institutions run into difficulties when it comes to finding specialists for the daily maintenance of their IT systems. Nevertheless, in the context of Euro-Atlantic integration, the academic community is involved in several important regional projects that are financed by the European Commission. These projects represent a step forward for the scientific research in the Balkans and neighbor countries. The following are some of the concrete examples connecting Balkan's national education research networks with the pan-European network education research giant.

- The See-grid and Seegrid2 projects also intend to develop and transmit the outcomes of grid technologies in the southeast European region, considered an important component in the European research area. Grid technologies enable the use of pan-European education research resources through participation in virtual research European organizations. The national academic network (education research) project that is financed by the Italian government is also of paramount importance.

- Besides new technologies and applications, fP7 foresees the continuation of giant, the multi-year project that establishes links among national academic networks with the pan-European network as well as networks from other communities. The current national program for research and development of IT with a time frame 2007–2009 attempts to encourage new IT usage and developments based on governmental objectives, achievements, and current international developments.

Role of e-government initiatives. The electronic government is a long process that goes through stages such as electronic information dissemination through a web presence up to the total transformation of the governance through the process of offering reliable, secure, easily accessible, public services online with an active participation of citizens and businesses. Electronic government in Albania is still in its early stages and some of the achievements so far are:

The government network Govnet, made possible through the support of UNDP and European Commission, is operational. Thanks to this project, the ministries, Departments of the Albanian government and two public service organizations (altogether 26 institutions) are interconnected through a high speed fiber-optic network.

The national agency for information society (NAIS) has carried out an evaluation of the existing IT infrastructure within the central administration and identified areas of improvement. Thanks to the establishment of a stable ICT policy, strong political commitment towards investing in the sector and the founding of NAIS Albania managed to launch its e-governance program ahead of schedule. The "Digital Albania Program" was set up together with the i2010 EU initiative and is likely to lead to further over-achievement by 2015.

Different successful projects for e-services in government, such as public electronic procurement, e-taxation, IS in customs (ASICUDA), have impacted the requirements for different products and services from the ICT sector. In fact, government leadership for the development of ICT sector has been in high levels in the recent years, showing the government will to do better in this field.

Although progress has been made towards the electronic government a number of problems and needs require further improvement:

- Increased awareness and knowledge across the public administration regarding the importance of the information technology in the process of electronic government and good governance
- Improvement of the information technology infrastructure in the public administration
- Standard definition with the aim of increasing effectiveness at work and lower operational costs
- Increase of information technology capacities and human resources and their continuous upgrading of the skills

5.2 Human Capacity Building in Albania

5.2.1 e-Education and Digital Literacy

Actually, there are 465,000 primary and secondary school students and 65,000 high school students in Albania. There are approximately 2,900 primary schools and about 522 high schools. This amounts to an average of less than a primary school per village and a little more than one high school in every commune.

Considering the status of ICT in Albanian schools, the situation is improved during last years, but still it is inadequate. In June 2002, about 500 PCs are available in 400 high schools, and only 25 high schools have a computer laboratory with ten computers each. In the course of the IT master plan implementation, there are 732 currently functioning computer labs in schools out of which 353 were built in the year 2008. In 37 high schools, there are two computer labs, 18 schools use the Internet service arranged for independently. Currently, there is one computer for 45 students.

Another very important project, the "Computerization of high school student's records" was also completed in 2007. This allows the creation of a comprehensive data base including all the students' records. The computerization of the "Primary/ secondary schools" was completed by 2009.

For the high school system, 2000 digital projectors and 2000 laptops were purchased, with the intention of using the equipment in mobile labs for teaching additional subjects.

All the universities have currently their internal computer networks and the Internet service is arranged independently. Computer equipment in a large number of universities is scarce and worn out. A teleconferencing project among the universities has already been envisaged through the cooperation of MASH (ministry of science and education) Italian Cooperation and specialists involved in scientific research. This network will provide them with the means for information exchange in scientific research for domains across the board.

There are different curricula in ICT field in higher level of education, professional education and in university level. Specialized training and/or certification on ICT are developing also. Anyway data are not available for the trainees in these programs.

The table below shows the empirical data about the factors listed, except for those that cannot be quantified, or at least for those that from statistical data in Albania could not be quantified.

5.2.2 Public and Business IT Education

The progress made up to now, regarding the increase of the number of Internet users, demonstrates among other things an increase in the level of awareness of the public with respect to the benefits and possibilities offered by ICTs.

At the same time, an increase has been experienced in the use of ICTs especially by large businesses. Nevertheless, the Internet penetration remains at low levels. One of the reasons is the low level of IT knowledge as well as the benefits that the use of the information and communication technology has to offer. The measures taken for the introduction of IT-related learning in the education system should be associated with education plans for the population at large that in one way or another would turn it into a wider usage of information or electronic services. The education of small and medium enterprises (SME) should be given a special importance due to the benefits and opportunities that the IT has to offer. The obligation to bestow special interest for the education of small and medium enterprises is based on the special role that the SME sector has for Albania, bearing in mind that especially the role of the micro-enterprises is considerable given the fact that they employ 77 % of the workforce. Micro-enterprises in Albania constitute about 95 % of the total number of enterprises, compared to 92 % in the overall European structure and they employ 42 % of the workforce.

5.2.3   Enterprise and e-Business

The electronic business is related to electronic commerce and a new way of operating for the enterprises through the active usage of ICT as well as the computerization of the businesses processes. In order to create an encouraging climate for the business, the government has undertaken a regulatory reform that has yielded the first results among which we could mention the establishment of the national Center for the registration of Businesses and the formulation of the law for the digital signatures.

Business registration is now achieved at the National Center for the registration of Business and considerable improvement has been made regarding the time of business registration reducing it from 42 days to 1 day. This center started its activity in September 2007 by offering:

1. "one-stop-shop" solutions for business registration
2. Electronic registration
3. Electronic Commercial register
4. Potential registration across Albania (ongoing)
5. Fulfillment of international standards for business registration
6. Many benefits and assistance for businesses.

Based on a survey carried out by IDA in 300 big companies, it was concluded that 84 % of the companies polled have full Internet access in their offices, 68 % of those businesses have broadband, and 58 % of the businesses have Intranets in their offices.

This is a considerable amount that demonstrates that an infrastructure for the use of the IT services is already in place. Nevertheless, it is worth mentioning that for the "Biggest taxpayers" that tend to be more consolidated financially and have well-organized administrative staff the cost is not an issue. Meantime, there is no actual evaluation for the Internet use by SME according to the study report of the observer for small and medium enterprises in Albania, prepared by the Center for research and development, (December 2006), a tendency by SME is emerging in recent years to invest in modernizing and introduction of new technologies.

The latest developments in infrastructure have given also some specific sectors, like the banking, an impetus to tackle the challenges encountered in offering these services. The security of the services offered by the banks and the cost transparency are essential important factors to be reckoned with.

5.2.4   Financial Forces and Prices

With increasing competition from new providers and services, telecommunications sector is becoming more mobile. Revenues from traditional services are under pressure from competitive providers and new distribution models. The role of speculative financial markets has increased.

These changes are threatening the financial health of many existing operators. Historically, they have maintained high prices for long distance and international services and have used them to sustain prices below cost for basic services. This pricing structure is generally supported by the adjusted agreements. With increasing competitive pressure on their prices even higher, these operators cannot rely any more on regulatory arrangements for basic services at low prices.

In addition, existing operators are facing significant cost investment to improve infrastructure to stay in pace with technological change. Success at this point would give competitive advantage in the long run. This scenario can lead to erosion of the value of existing assets (often state owned). With increasing competitive pressure, regulators need to justify the price policy aimed at keeping prices low basic services and review the tariff rebalance for reflecting better the economic costs.

5.3   Infrastructure of Information and Communication Technology

The national ICT infrastructure is the main pillar of the information society. In a wider sense, it includes wire-based, wireless telecommunications, satellite, computer networks, transmission and commutation systems, digital television, a wide range of terminal devices, software programs and applications, electronic data bases and digital libraries.

As stated also in the literature review, basic infrastructure to be reviewed includes:

- Fixed telephony
- Mobile telephony and
- Internet Access

It seems that the general condition of Albania's fixed line is not good compared to other countries. Thus, the penetration level is slightly higher than the country ranked last in the region of SEE, Kosovo, and is far by being a very good penetration level of over 95 % of the population with access to fixed telephony, as in other countries, Serbia, Croatia, Macedonia, BHZ.

The telecommunications sector in Albania has been liberalized and the number of operators that operate in this field has increased significantly. The national operator for the fixed lines public services, Alb Telecom Ltd. was privatized (76 %) in 2007. Alb telecom has a nationwide infrastructure with a transmission and switching system almost fully digitalized. This operator also offers dial-up Internet service in towns countrywide and ADSL in the main cities although the cost of this service is relatively high. The landline penetration remains quite low and by the end of 2007 it was estimated at 10 %. This reduces opportunities to benefit from broadband services such as LLU and the lack of competition in offering xDSL is another impediment that leads to higher rates for the offering of these services.

The indicator of the spread of mobile telephony has more or less the same development of this subsector, with 2–3 operators who display almost the same degree of competition. The operators of mobile phone services AMC and Vodafone Albania have grown significantly during the period 2001–2007 by increasing as a result the mobile phone penetration over 70 % (see footnote 1 in Chap. 1). Studies (see footnote 2 in Chap. 1) show that prices of services offered are higher compared to other countries in the region. The entrance of the third operator, Eagle mobile, in 2008, increased competition and had a positive impact by providing benefits for the consumers. The fourth operator that has entered the market in the past three years, has influenced the decrease of the market prices. Mobile phone operators offer GPRS and Edge services. GPRS is enabled across the country where mobile phone coverage is available, whereas Edge is offered only partially. Although those services may be considered as expensive, the charges applied are based on transfer rates and are cost-effective for low transaction applications.

Starting in year 2000, several public telecommunications entities launched operations in rural areas by offering services in communes, which was the smallest licensing zone. Although their number grew year over year, legal restraints limiting the offering of services only in rural areas did not produce considerable results in fixed line penetration in those areas or any tangible improvements in infrastructure. Nevertheless based on the number of phone users, those operators control about 11 % of the fixed line market in the country. Legal changes effectuated by the end of 2006, enabled these operators to offer phone services in urban and interurban areas based on the principle of technological neutrality. The number of the alternative operators offering local and regional fixed line services is 61.

Albania has a considerable number of ISPs taking into account the small area of the country. The number of Internet service providers (ISP) has grown significantly. The number of licensed operators by the telecommunications regulatory entity was 32 (see footnote 5 in Chap. 1) one of which was offering backbone services, 15 national ISPs, 2 regional, 9 local, and 5 PoPs. Among the biggest ISPs, we could mention: Abcom, Albania online, Abissnet, Alb telecom, Pronet, etc. The number of Internet users is given in the table with the statistics in the next section.

5.4   Infrastructure and Access, Services, and Technologies in ICT Sector

It was mentioned previously in this work that the Information Society infrastructures are supplied by the ICT sector. Despite the fact that the Albanian ICT sector has achieved much in its development in the last few years, there still are a few technological needs to be covered such as the countrywide Internet coverage and a faster and more reliable network infrastructure.

Even though the increasing level of the indicators such as penetration of fixed lines and Internet, the percentage of PC ownership, costs of Internet and mobile access and services, the figures remain low in relation to the world standards, and other countries' infrastructures. Still Albania has succeeded in increasing substantially its investments in the ICT sector. A considerable growth in the availability of e-services across most basic government services is being noticed in the last years— almost 80 % of the basic e-government services at the central government level are currently accessible.

Having in mind that through introducing broadband networks and services strong economic growth and increased competitiveness can be achieved, one of the main targets of the Albanian government is the building of a national, wireless broadband network which will provide Internet to all public schools, academic institutions, government agencies, and the Albanian citizenry in general. The installation of this network will foster Albania's further modernization and economic, social, cultural, and political integration.

In the last few years, Albania has achieved a considerable progress in the development of its ICT infrastructure but still lags behind its neighboring countries in terms of introducing new technologies such as 3G mobile, DSL, cable TV, and WiMax. For example, Albania was the only country in Europe (in addition to Kosovo) that had yet to issue a 3G license, but in January 2011, Vodafone Albania launched the country's first 3G network with coverage that will initially be available only on the territory of the capital city of Tirana.[1]

A progress that is worth mentioning is in the area of mobile communications which was developed and improved to one of the best levels in the region. Since 2009 till today, there are four mobile operators in Albania which highly stimulated competition and brought Albania a mobile penetration rate of 135 % in 2010. It is expected to grow more and more in the next couple of years as the mobile networks are now expanding in rural areas looking for more customers.

In fact, infrastructure development is related directly with the development of ICT sector in Albania.

The electronic readiness indicators ranked Albania among the last countries polled in 2005, while in the recent years, as discussed in the previous section, Albania has done considerable progress, being ranked in the middle, but still remaining in the

---

[1] ICT country profile: ALBANIA 2.

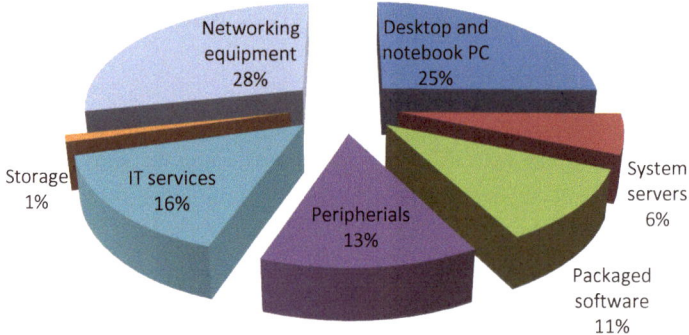

Fig. 5.1   Market shares of different segments fo ICT market, 2008

last positions within the SEE countries. The development in ranking is due to the progress in the ICT market.[2]

Most of the companies working in the ICT market in Albania are not specialized in a particular market segment but have two or more activities in their portfolio. Very few companies are specialized, for example, only in software development, design, system integration, or hardware distribution. As the main market of the local companies is mainly the domestic one the companies have to adjust their specializations in wider aspects. Most of their products and services are built upon their customers requirements, but still they possess and develop their own products and services in different fields.[3]

According to the IDC[4] study of Albanian IT market, the last figures publicly available are those of 2008 and 2009. Market shares of different segments in this market are illustrated below in Figs. 5.1 and 5.2. The figures of 2008 reflect the notable market structure changes from the prior year: the shares of IT services and packaged software of the overall IT market grew considerably—at the expense of the hardware share.[5]

On the other hand, from the comparison between Figs. 5.1 and 5.2, it can be seen that almost all the segments are declining while the segment that is raising in its market value is that of networking equipment. This is due to the raising importance of networking. But it has to be mentioned that the value of the market has been declining for the years 2009–2010 because of the crisis effects. In fact, Fig. 5.3 shows the forecast of IT market before and after the predictions of the crisis, while Fig. 5.4 shows

---

[2] *INSTAT, LSMS 2002, IT Market Analyses Study.*

[3] http://intra.undp.org.al/ext/elib/download/?id=1058&name=Albania%20National%20MDG%20 Report%20%2D%20July%202010%

[4] IDC is the only international IT market research and consulting firm with research facilities throughout the Central and Eastern Europe, Middle East and Africa region (CEMA), as well as Research Centers devoted exclusively to tracking the fast evolving IT markets of this region (Prague, Czech Republic—CEE; Dubai, UAE—MEA).

[5] IDC market study 2008

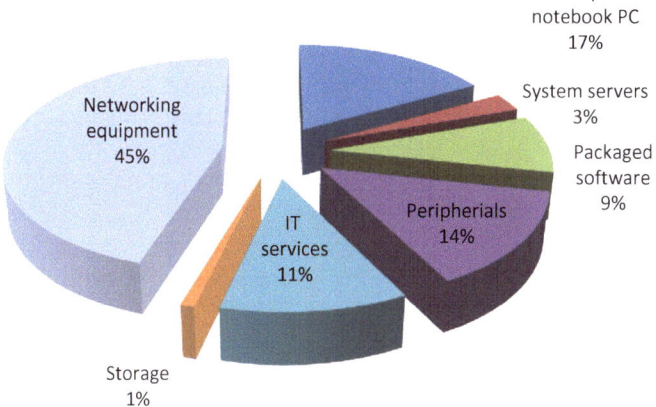

Fig. 5.2 Segments in ICT market in 2009

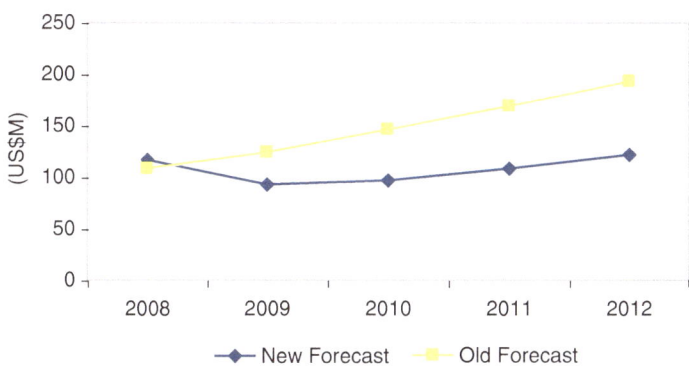

Fig. 5.3 Forecasts of the IT market according to IDC market study 2008

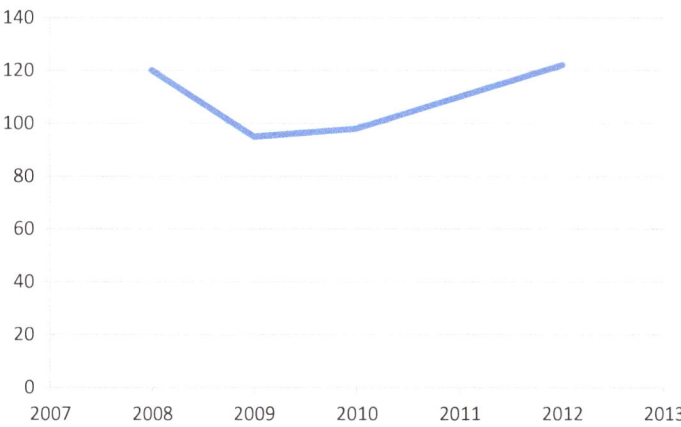

Fig. 5.4 Actual sales in IT market in Albania

the actual data about this market. It is clear that the real situation of the IT market in 2009–2010 has been lower than predicted in both situations, but the market is still raising in the last 2 years, although, not in the same figures as in IDC forecasts.

This progress in the market value as well as other indicators represented in Table 5.1. In fact, the figures show the evolution reflected in only some of the indicators. Some important data are missing, not only for some of the years, but also for other indicators, such as number of firms in ICT, number of computers for 100 inhabitants, trainees in ICT field or expenditures in import–export in ICT. Some data are missing because of the statistics system, which gives only the data for post and communication, but does not see the ICT sector as a separated sector for the purpose of gathering statistics. The agencies mentioned above, created for the purpose of building and fostering ICT sector and information society, have gathered data only in the recent years, but data are missing from previous years:

•   A great number of companies have been established in its related activities. Even though there are not reliable data about a trend in the number of companies, from different data sources, there are 99 IT companies in 2008, 152 companies in 2009, while this number has increased in almost 200 in 2012.

•   The number of computers per 100 inhabitants increased from 0.5 in 2002 to 1.2 in the year 2005,[6] thus a 250 % increase. According to INSTAT (Albanian statistics institute), the number of computers in the country is estimated at 85.000 (2005), but there is not a reliable figure in the last years. The IDC study shows that about half are used by the private entities and public administration. In fact, the ITU statistics shows us only about the percentage of households with computers, and with Internet access as shown in Table 5.1

•   The number of Internet users per 100 inhabitants has raised dramatically from 0.39 in 2002, to 6 in 2005 and to 55 in 2012 (in 2000 it was estimated at about 2000 Internet users, in a population of almost three million people), according to the information technology statistics published by ITU.[7] This number indicates a considerable number of Internet users; still the penetration remains low in this factor. According to the nonofficial data provided by some Internet service provider, the growth of the Internet users in recent years in estimated at 30–40 %. Despite this indicator, the largest clients and users of the Internet remain the state institutions and large companies.

The number of registered domains has also known an upward trend year over year. The total number of active domains registered by the end of 2007 was 729.

The growing tendency in the IT sector is reflected in the evaluation conducted in the framework of the project score-project. Eu, which notes: "the majority of the products is imported. Nevertheless, there is a strong growing tendency in the IT sector to adapt the products to local needs. Some of the programs are customized in the

---

[6] INSTAT, LSMS 2005

[7] http://www.itu.int/ITU-D/ict/newslog/Vodafone+Launches+Its+3G+Network+In+Albania.aspx

Table 5.1 Indicators of the model for the development of ICT market

Group			II. Human factor				III Entrepreneurship			IV access and infrastructure					V ICT sector		
Years	Number of companies in ICT sector	Government expenditures in ICT	Number of students in ICT field	Gross enrolment ratio secondary (%)	Gross enrolment ratio tertiary (%)	Percentage of Individuals using Internet	Lending level of economy	Telecommunication investment commitments	FDI in communications	Fixed telephone subscription per 100 inhabitants	Mobile subscription per 100 inhabitants	Internet bandwidth (bits/ Internet user	Percentage of households with Internet access	Percentage of households with computer	Fixed wired broadband subscription per 100 inhabitants	Total revenues (million leke)	Market value in million leke
2000										4.97							
2001										6.42							
2002			235	73	15.8	0.39				7.12	27.54	1,000	1	2			
2003		201.152	879			0.97	52,309.19			8.21	35.41						
2004		222.438	1.236			2.42	71,705.63			8.79	40.31						
2005		232.340	1.456			6.04	124,427.73			8.88	48.71	1,164		1.2	0.01	11.000	59.000
2006		258.816	2.675			9.61	195,746.79	337.666		8.11	60.5	1,461				13.000	26.101
2007		285.675	2.345	79.8	32.2	15.04	293,863.70	1,622.203	554.88	9.46	73.27	1,581	7.8	9.5	0.32	16,453	75.980
2008	99	351.491	2.987	78.7	36.7	23.86	396,264.33	1,322.202	349.93	9.46	58.45	1,956	8.8	12	2.01	18.976	120.000
2009	152	379.861		72.4	36.7	41.2	440,397.35		315.58	10.8	77.17	9,709	9	13	2.88		94.897
2010		362.752		88.9	36.7	45	483,129.68		360.68	11.37	84.02	11.790	13.7	15.6	3.29	57.120	98.234
2011		376.353		88.9	36.7	49	541,899.76		350.89	10.54	96.39	19,038	15.7	16.4	3.99		110.103
2012	200	301.551				54.66	554,713.88			9.67	108.45				4.96		122.119

local language. There is a multitude of choices with respect to devices and programs, which are easily accessible and affordable to the majority of small and medium enterprises as well as individuals."

The information technology-related revenues are also raising as shown in the data of Table 5.1.

The Albanian IT market continued its dynamic growth in 2008, with total spending reaching $117.25 million, but went in lower levels in 2009–2010, with around 20 % decline. In fact in the last two years, data show that IT market is growing very slowly. The IT spending surge in Albania can be largely attributed to the public sector demand—the government's technology procurements more than doubled from the previous year. Other IT market drivers included continuously increasing technology investments in the finance and telecoms sectors and falling equipment prices. IT spending in the country was supported by a robust economy, including increased household disposable income due to expanding credit.

While IT services-related revenue and packaged software shipments surged, hardware sales recorded a lower growth rate than the market average in these years.

In terms of the global economic crisis, although the negative impacts on IT spending in Albania were evident only in 2009–2010.

As international and regional vendors enter the Albanian IT market, local IT vendors must evaluate their ability to compete in terms of staff (quality and number of certified engineers and technicians, as well as strong management), finances, and marketing. Achieving a sizeable client base, by partnering or merging, will be crucial in winning larger projects and strengthening market position. Local IT vendors should reevaluate their growth strategies, try to find niches not of interest to large vendors, and differentiate and brand themselves. They should also leverage their flexibility, local market and language expertise, and competitive pricing.

Speaking about companies in ICT market, Infosoft Systems remains the leader in terms of providing Information Technology services in the Albanian market. This is the conclusion published by IDC in a special study that the company has implemented the "IT Market Forecast in Albania 2012–2016 and sales rankings for 2011." According to the study, in 2011, the Information Technology market in Albania has increased by 5.5 % year on year to 190.43 million dollars quota. Findings in the IDC show that Infosoft Systems already owns 22.9 % of the market. Lately, there has been successfully completed two of the four major projects for Software in 2011 as: "Procurement and delivery of software applications flee the Ministry of Labour and Social Affairs" and "Maintaining and improving the resolution of the National Agency eCabinet Information Society."

The IT market in 2012 and beyond can be expected to grow slowly. IDC believes that the costs for the purposes of Information Technology in Albania will grow by 2.5 % per year in 2012. For the remaining period (2013–2016), IDC predicts a slight increase. Expected a slowdown in mobile type and distribution of IT Network equipment, while traditional ingredients IT (IT servers, software, computers, and peripherals hardcopy) will stay at very best.

The data will be tested in the linear multiple regression model to find if there is a direct or indirect relationship between all the variables. So, in the model we will test the relationship between market value of ICT sector or total revenues in ICT sector as dependent variables (Y), and all the other variables in Table 5.1 as dependent variables.

In previous work, we have shown only some of these relationships. Actually, all the statistics gathered from national and international bodies and agencies and their reports make it possible to broaden the study and show which factors have affected mostly the development of ICT market in Albania, during the last years. From the data we can see that there are missing vales that do not allow us to test some of the relationships, but it is important to give the interested reader an idea of the problems that exist with data and statistics. We can mention as such variables are:

- Number of companies in the sector, an indicator included in the study for showing the competition in the market,
- Number of students in ICT field, trying to show the human capacities. The data are gathered from direct sources, universities, and departments, but not for the last years. Also the data gathered may be not very reliable because no formal statistics exists for the specific brunches,
- Telecommunication investments commitments, an indicator that shows for the engagement of firms and companies in the light of entrepreneurship. Data are missing in this indicator for the same reasons above.

Another problem that must be mentioned is that some other indicators found in our study, that may be a proper representation of the forces, do not have data at all. These include mostly the first group of forces, where we can mention the ICT exports and ICT imports, public funding for research projects in ICT, number of e-services users.

Some factors are, on the other hand qualitative, where can be mentioned the intellectual property laws, security and privacy, technological standards. These forces are analyzed in the previous section, mostly in the light of legislation and the government initiatives for the development of ICT market.

Testing the data will take place in two phases, since there are a great number of independent variables. So the first phase will include the identification of the indicator that is the most important inside of that group of forces. The second phase will test the most important factors from all the forces, as explained later on in this section.

The model for predicting the most important independent variables is the linear regression $Y = \beta 0 + \beta_1 X_1 + \beta_2 X_2 + \ldots \beta_n X_n + \in$. The data will be tested according to the number of variables in each group as explained below.

For the first group, there are only two quantitative variables, of which only Government expenses in ICT[8] is an available indicator for this group. Even from the tests, this remains the only possible variable to be included from the first group.

---

[8] Data source is Bank of Albania (data are taken only for the purpose of this study, and do not exist in any formal document, or report.

People skills for effective use of ICT, where the representative indicators are: the number of graduates over the years in the field of ICT, secondary and tertiary gross enrolment rates. There are no data on the number of trainees in various ways related to ICT, even there are some related projects about trainings as explained in the previous. The other variables are included as explained in the measurement of information society reports, as the use component of the IDI, since the enrolment rates affect also the digital literacy among population. But they can be considered as affecting in an indirect way the development of ICT sector. Another important variable in the use component is also the percentage of Internet users. In fact, this is a real indicator about the digital literacy among Albanian population.

The tests for the three variables of the second group show that enrolment rates are not important variables, they are excluded from the model, along with the number of students. The missing values may have affected this model, but since there are data for 6 years, we may rely on this analysis. The predictor in the second group of variables, as shown in the ANNEX 2 from the SPSS tests, is the percentage of Internet users. This use component is the variable that will be considered in the second phase as representative of the human forces impact in ICT sector.

Entrepreneurship is represented by three important indicators, being the lending level in the Albanian economy to represent the access to capital, Foreign Direct Investments in telecommunications and investments commitment of companies in telecommunications. In fact, these are the only data that can be reliable because telecommunication is the segment within ICT that have the most investments, also according to AKEP and other reports, while the investments in other companies are not shown. Tests for the three variables show that the only predictor remains FDI. Data show a negative relationship between them and the market value of ICT/revenues in ICT market.

Infrastructure and access is the third group of factors that are represented by several indicators such as number of fixed and mobile subscriptions per 100 inhabitants, Internet bandwidth, percentage of households with computers and Internet access. As widely explained earlier in this study, these indicators provide users the opportunity to access ICT. In fact, there are a number of other indicators that would point out any better in aspects of infrastructure development in the telecommunications market, but as previously mentioned, there is a significant lack of data on these indicators, such as the number of secure Internet servers and the number of access points per 100 inhabitants.

After the first phase tests, the second phase included the tests for five variables, each of the most important variables of each group, experimented in the first phase, as mentioned above, they were the Government expenditures in ICT ($X1$), Percentage of Internet users ($X2$), FDI in communications ($X3$), mobile subscriptions for 100 inhabitants ($X4$), percentage of households with computers ($X5$). The testing shows that the predictors of the model are Government expenditures in ICT and Mobile subscriptions for 100 inhabitants. The most important is mobile subscriptions per 100 inhabitants.

We try to use a fifth degree model:

$$Y = \beta0 + \beta1X1 + \beta2X2 + \beta3X3 + \beta4X4 + \beta5X5 + \in$$

After testing the model with the data with SPSS.17, we reduce the number of independent variables in two, because all the tests done with five independent variables, exclude from the model always three of them. The testing shows that the predictors of the model are Government expenditures in ICT and Mobile subscriptions for 100 inhabitants. The most important is mobile subscriptions per 100 inhabitants.

So the model is restricted in two independent variables for the revenues in ICT sector:

$$Y = \beta 0 + \beta 1 X 1 + \beta 5 X 5 + \in$$

The tests with market value of ICT show also a positive relationship with the percentage of households with computers and FDI in communications, predicting a model with four variables as shown in Annex 2.

Chapter 6
Conclusions and Recommendations

Nowadays, the economy and society as a whole is relying more and more on the spread and use of information as a core element of their development. Information is becoming important not only for individual lives, but mostly for companies success, sector and market developments, and then for the development of country economies in today's global markets. Another element related today more than ever with information is communication. People communicate not only for the simple purpose of transmitting messages, but for exchanging information, which has become in a lot of aspects the reason for communicating, especially in an economic aspect.

Economies and countries, more eager for relying on information are requiring more ICTs as the only mean that can support the development of the society in the light of information and communication importance. So, the spread of ICTs is becoming a core element of the development of economies, contributing in a different stage not only of their development, but also in the development of the societies. The term information society is now defining this new stage, where societies do not rely only on production or consumption, or services, but mostly in the spread and use of information for the purpose of development, job and wealth creation, value added in the economy.

These new trends were lying behind the reasons of this study, which tried to deeply analyze the most important elements which affect the development of information society in the right direction. As our first goal was to bring to the reader more insight in the concept of Information Society and the elements underlying this concept, at the very end we can say that information society is a stage of development of a society strongly related with the economy that has the following characteristics:

1. Use of information and knowledge
2. Economic and technologic transformations
3. Use of ICTs
4. New economic methods and models
5. Demand for new professions
6. Change in business landscape

© The Author(s) 2015   85
E. Kordha Tolica et al., *Information Society Development through ICT Market Strategies*, SpringerBriefs in Business, DOI 10.1007/978-3-319-17196-8_6

Dealing with these changes requires a new vision for the development of a country and a strategy for achieving the stage of information society because the purpose should be to derive economic and social benefits from these new trends. This vision and strategy must include the use of rapid transformation in ICTs for improving peoples' lives through ICT use in the long term. This is possible only through a strategic vision for the economic impact which must include measurable outcomes and benchmarking over a given time frame.

The development of strategies for the information society has become a must in different countries since there are also regional strategies and those in the EU level that try to give a proper direction in the development of information societies. Strategy development need also the right measurements and the knowledge of the level of preparation of a country for IS development, in order to achieve the maximum economic and other benefits from the use of digital technology. The notion of preparation leads to the concept of e-readiness, which is one of the elements that characterize the information society.

e-Readiness is about readiness in human capacities, political leadership, institutional frameworks, supportive policies, complementary regulations, business environment, investment opportunities, and public–private partnerships in technologies. A review of recent experiences in the developing world shows that the countries which are the most successful in creating a favorable climate for the use of ICTs are those that make it a priority.

The success required from ICT strategy implementation affects and is affected from ICT facilities quality and information system quality. In turn, they affect the perceived benefits. An ICT project implementation can only be perceived to have succeeded if the perceived benefits are realized. ICT facilities quality can be assessed after careful evaluation of the infrastructure to determine technical functionality.

So, the physical infrastructure of Information Systems is one of the important components of the information society. From this perspective the basic infrastructures as well as the related services are object of the first assessments of e-readiness in different countries.

Another aspect of this work deals with the identification of the indicators to be used. After an attentive look of different methods, we conclude that the distinction between measurements of use, access, and impact is very important. Access indicators measure what people or businesses have in terms of ICTs or how many exist in a country. Usage indicators measure how and for what ICTs are being used by households, individuals, businesses or governments, etc. Impact indicators capture the impact of access and usage on economic growth, employment creation, improvement in public service delivery on a macro level; and company performance, household poverty levels and social inclusion on a micro level, to give just a few examples. Impact indicators are usually derived from analysis of primary or secondary data.

For the purpose of this study, we focused on access indicators and in some extent in use indicators and for this reason we studied the ICT sector and market in details. After a thorough examination of definitions and history of ICT sector, we conclude that the product/service in the ICT sector is the core of information society infrastructure. To be more concrete, ICT are a collection of technologies and applications that enable the processing, storage, and electronic transfer of information to a multiple user or customer. These technologies and applications are further classified into three categories based on their use: (1) computing (2) communication, and (3) Internet—the possibility of communication and computation. The two most important aspects of ICTs are the main processes and communications **infrastructure**. Communication processes can be one- or two sided. The relatively new technology of communication involves a number of nets that connect to each other through electronic communication. The Internet represents the convergence of communication and computation as well as spinal forms of economy and information society. Substantial improvements in strength, speed of computation and storage or total capacity, have greatly encouraged the development of economy and society based on information and knowledge. New technologies include so, hardware, software, and services in various fields. They include government, business, entertainment and art, science and medicine as well as knowledge management and distribution among multiple applications.

The sense of the product/services of ICT sector affects both the access infrastructures needed for the IS development and the measurement of market value and revenues of companies that of ICT. Analyzing the sector requires reliable data from government institutions and the awareness of ICT companies to take part in the measurement process since they are providing with the necessary infrastructures for the information economy and society. The accessibility and reliability of such infrastructure is assuming a great importance to the knowledge-based economy and society. Indeed one of the most important becoming infrastructures is also the supply of broadband services.

After a discussion of infrastructures in developed countries, it is understood that they have relied in their strategies more on free market forces, but the lack of government leadership has led to calls for governments to reassert themselves in this policy field through such means as regulatory reform and renewed public investment. Their experience shows that the role of municipalities and communities could also be very important in constructing their networks, as core elements in infrastructures of a country.

But the vision and the strategy designed in different countries depend on their context, so it is different in developing and developed countries. In fact, one of the questions raised at the beginning of this study was whether the information society will be built relying more on public efforts, or private sector.

We can say that market forces alone cannot make a difference, but even counting only on government leadership and public actors' efforts is not the best solution for building the information society. In fact, the initial enthusiasm for the development of ICT has already been replaced by caution that without focusing on all elements influencing, only the introduction of new technologies, will not provide the expected promised development.

Many governments, especially those of developing countries including Albania, are seeking to promote economic growth by assisting in the emergence and growth of local ICT industries. In this context, an important role in achieving growth and productivity in the ICT sector will play all the factors which influence the growth and development of this market.

A nation's regulatory policies can have a profound influence on ICT investment and use. Where a nation's legal framework offers strong incentives for people to develop and acquire ICTs—including the skills necessary to use ICTs effectively—governments will have greater success in leveraging the power of ICTs and ICT industrial growth to advance social and economic development goals.

After reviewing each of the above factors for the development of ICT sector in Albania several important conclusions for each of the factors influencing arise from qualitative research and empirical data that lead analysis a step further.

ICTs are finding today in the Albanian society, a steadily increasing use, for the Albanian Government has established and implements the national strategy for ICTs.

Concerning the legal framework which is needed in order to facilitate and support the implementation and improvement of new technologies, new services and new regulations in the Albanian ICT sector little is left to be done, as most of the basic requirements for success in this field have been fulfilled. The regulatory framework for ICTs is not very updated in accordance with the European Union standards but however much work is under process.

> *ICTs are now used more in sectors such as governance and administration, but also education and business. They are used less in health or other sectors. There is still much to do, although ongoing efforts are taking place for its nationwide expansion.*

Some important findings show about the growth of users of Internet and mobile phones, as well as the number of graduate students in ICT curricula around the country. Beyond the actual use, digital literacy means more. Increased use will come from more education and trainings in ICT. But, efforts to improve in this regard are also scarce. A low percentage of organizations subject to the interviewing through their managers/owners to train employees train their employees in the field of computer science, compared to the percentage of those who do not train.

It can be asserted that ICTs have just started to have a bigger attention from the business community and Albanian government as well. However, there is still to be done in terms of ICT infrastructure development and ICT SME usage promotion. Without a modern ICT infrastructure, the business community will find itself behind their regional competitors and will not be ready to fully cooperate regionally or internationally.

Big enterprises have started to adopt e-learning training tools for their staff and there is a good sign that this will increase in the near term. The majority part of small and medium business fully understands the benefits of ICT usage but they lack the proper funding and facilities to apply ICT in their premises.

The *e-Albania* campaign that includes the most important activities and services in the country such as e-health, e-government, e-schools, e-business, e-commerce, e-tax, and e-procurement should be more reactive and should involve more small and medium enterprises in terms of seminars, workshops, conferences, and trainings.

Albania should seriously consider the need of investments in building high capacity optical fiber terrestrial backbone infrastructure in order to support the building and delivery of a broadband Internet network. Albtelecom is still the only operator with national and international connections available but still has a very limited coverage. With the help of more investments in infrastructure and more preliminary construction planning of pipes and ducts in new roads, a lot can be done to improve the urban, interurban, and international connections.

The main infrastructural issues to be covered are the penetration of fixed lines and Internet, the percentage of PC ownership, costs of Internet and mobile access and services, low level of awareness of the benefits of the use of ICTs, digital gap between urban and rural areas and in comparison to other countries in Europe, low level of state subsidies and lack of policies to support all these.

The ICT market was declining during the last years because of the crisis as stated by IDC. But it is foreseen that when the crisis will slowly begin to recede, the country will gradually achieve positive GDP growth, and the ICT market will return to solid annual growth rates.

But, on the other hand, it must be admitted that there are some problems which need to face Albania for the development and use of these technologies. As seen from the description of the general economic framework of Albania, to bear in mind some limitations connected with the overall situation. These include:

- High social inequalities in the country with a relatively unfamiliar with computers and technology and lack of knowledge of English language, from a part of population
- Lack of funds to a significant fraction of the population to ensure access to ICT
- Problems of lack of proper infrastructure for the access of the population at appropriate levels.

Some of the opportunities of Albania related to factors that impact positively on development and growth of ICT sector are:

- Excellent human resources in terms of specialists
- Has experienced growth in important sectors of the economy, as the construction sector of trade
- Number of businesses born each year, business structures
- Continued growth rates of lending to the economy, etc.

The e-readiness assessment provides all the information regarding the constraints and obstacles to a swift development of ICTs. Such constraints and obstacles are in fact an invitation to action, and it is the role of the strategy to define how to overcome them. Measurements of information society and e-readiness in Albania put Albania in middle ranking in a world level, but in the last positions in the SEE region. Skills level of population is a positive factor affecting these positions better than world average, but access in ICT and their use still are putting Albania in low levels. According to network readiness, the problems remain mainly in business usage, infrastructure, and economic impact, where Albania has the lowest scores. But even in government usage and political regulatory environment, where our efforts have been considerable, the scores are not satisfiable. Albania should look at the experience of some of SEE countries that, even in somewhat similar conditions, have done significant progress especially in infrastructure and access and also in usage of ICTs. Their efforts in innovation, individual usage, and government usage are also higher.

Further on, the literature review showed that development of ICT sector depends on different forces that can be grouped in four categories: Innovation and government efforts, entrepreneurship, literacy, and use of ICT from human resources and infrastructure and access to ICT.

Our fifth degree model of linear regression test showed that some variables have not been important in Albanian case. In fact, the forces that the most have drown the development and growth of ICT market in Albania in last 8–10 years are the government efforts and the evolution of the mobile market, through the strong raise of mobile subscriptions. Other important factors are also those regarding Internet use and the capacity of investments in ICT.

After this study, some of the recommendations for policymakers, on strategies to promote an ICT-based growth for an information society, include:

- *Provide effective patent protection for ICTs*: Patents stimulate innovation by giving firms the means to protect new and useful technologies against misappropriation. The requirement that inventors publicly disclose their innovations as a condition of protection, combined with the widespread practice in the ICT sector of cross-licensing patented innovations to third parties, promote the diffusion of technical knowledge and spur follow-on innovation by subsequent inventors. Inventions that otherwise meet the criteria for patentability should not be denied protection merely because they are implemented in computers or other ICTs.
- *Policies must also take into consideration building a regulatory environment that supports microfinance*: An important complement to property ownership—and a critical element to the viability of business-to-consumer e-commerce—is straightforward, widespread access to microcredit and microfinance. Governments should also remove regulatory barriers that might impede financial institutions from offering credit cards and similar financing options to consumers, and should provide incentives and consumer protections to ensure that such credit options are available to underserved populations.
- Promote open, competitive trade in ICT products and services by implementing the policies that *incite market access for ICTs and cross-border e-commerce*: Government in developing countries, especially in Albania should ensure that the ICT market is not distorted by preferences for certain classes of producers, including those utilizing specific development or licensing models, should base ICT procurement decisions on relevant performance-related criteria such as value, total cost of ownership, feature set, performance, and security. While e-commerce allows vendors in developing countries to reach customers regardless of geographic location at low cost, thereby helping them compete effectively in the global marketplace. So proper e-commerce solutions would help business readiness which is lacking in Albania.

- *Encourage collaboration between public and private researchers*: Joint research ventures between publicly funded institutions (such as universities or other nonprofit research institutions) and ICT firms can provide an important financing mechanism for basic scientific research. Such collaboration can also shorten the time between the discovery of new technologies and their commercial application.
- *Provide incentives for ICT education and training at all levels*: Primary and secondary schools should offer ICT skills training and testing opportunities, and colleges and universities should be given incentives and additional resources for providing ICT skills training. ICT retraining and lifelong learning programs are also critically important to ensure that workers have the opportunity to strengthen their IT skills and thereby become more employable and productive.
- *Strengthening business education and training and including ICTs*: Lack of critical business skills may impede the emergence of a domestic, entrepreneurial ICT sector. Government and domestic business associations have major roles to play in providing a framework to encourage business skills development, *e.g.*, through vocational training and other training programs directed at improving the businesses of SMEs.
- *Support microfinance mechanisms*: Microfinance has proven to be an extremely effective development tool, although to date much of this financing has been provided through nonprofit organizations. Governments should foster microfinance-based initiatives and remove any regulatory obstacles that might impede access to such financing. In the longer term, governments should examine ways also to provide such financing through for-profit institutions so as to ensure that these mechanisms are sustainable.
- *Incentives for private-sector R&D and ICT spending*: Promoting a regulatory environment that values innovation and encourages ICT investment is vital to capitalizing on the potential of ICTs to promote development objectives. Tax credits and other incentives for private-sector R&D will foster innovation, while similar incentives for investments in telecommunications infrastructure will promote broad public access to the benefits of ICTs. To promote productivity growth, businesses and other organizations should be offered financial incentives to invest in ICTs and provide IT training to their employees. Examples of such incentives include tax credits, loans at favorable interest rates, and accelerated depreciation schedules for ICT assets.
- *Invest in targeted broadband network development*: Although universal broadband network access is likely to be prohibitively expensive in the short term, targeting specific industries or locales for broadband development may in certain cases be economically feasible and provide important benefits. For example, efforts to provide broadband access to technology parks or other areas with high concentrations of IT firms would stimulate IT sector development and serve as a model for broadband deployment more broadly.

Annex 1

Albana

Networked readiness index 2012	68	3.9
A. Environment subindex	82	3.7
1st pillar: Political and regulatory environment	89	3.5
2nd pillar: Business and innovation environment	78	3.9
B. Readiness subindex	65	4.8
3rd pillar: Infrastructure and digital content	75	3.7
4th pillar: Affordability	57	5.4
5th pillar: Skills	56	5.2
C. Usage subindex	62	3.7
6th pillar: Individual usage	59	3.6
7th pillar: Business usage	74	3.5
8th pillar: Government usage	64	3.9
D. Impact subindex	72	3.4
9th pillar: Economic impacts	75	3.2
10th pillar: Social impacts	69	3.7
The networked readiness index in detail		
1st pillar: Political and regulatory environment		
• 1.01 Effectiveness of law-making bodies*	63	3.6
• 1.02 Laws relating to ICT*	76	3.8
• 1.03 Judicial independence*	101	3.0
• 1.04 Efficiency of legal system in settling disputes*	63	3.7
• 1.05 Efficiency of legal system in challenging regs*	65	3.7
• 1.06 Intellectual property protection*	94	3.0
• 1.07 Software piracy rate, % software installed	77	75
• 1.08 No. of procedures to enforce a contract	87	39
• 1.09 No. of days to enforce a contract	26	390

(continued)

© The Author(s) 2015
E. Kordha Tolica et al., *Information Society Development through ICT Market Strategies*, SpringerBriefs in Business, DOI 10.1007/978-3-319-17196-8

(continued)

2nd pillar: Business and innovation environment		
• 2.01 Availability of latest technologies*	75	4.9
• 2.02 Venture capital availability*	124	2.0
• 2.03 Total tax rate, % profits	70	38.5
• 2.04 No. days to start a business	10	5
• 2.05 No. procedures to start a business	28	5
• 2.06 Intensity of local competition*	122	4.0
• 2.07 Tertiary education gross enrollment rate, %	94	18.4
• 2.08 Quality of management schools*	69	4.2
• 2.09 Gov't procurement of advanced tech*	58	3.8
3rd pillar: Infrastructure and digital content		
• 3.01 Electricity production, kWh/capita	91	1,193.5
• 3.02 Mobile network coverage, % pop	69	98.2
• 3.03 Int'l Internet bandwidth, kb/s per user	67	11.8
• 3.04 Secure Internet servers/million pop	90	8.4
• 3.05 Accessibility of digital content*	87	4.7
4th pillar: Affordability		
• 4.01 Mobile cellular tariffs, PPP $/min	96	0.42
• 4.02 Fixed broadband Internet tariffs, PPP $/month	39	25.34
• 4.03 Internet and telephony competition, 0–2 (best)	84	1.69
5th pillar: Skills		
• 5.01 Quality of educational system*	45	4.2
• 5.02 Quality of math and science education*	42	4.5
• 5.03 Secondary education gross enrollment rate, %	92	78.2
• 5.04 Adult literacy rate, %	59	95.9
6th pillar: Individual usage		
• 6.01 Mobile phone subscriptions/100 pop	19	
• 6.02 Individuals using Internet, %	55	
• 6.03 Households w/ personal computer, %	95	
• 6.04 Households w/ Internet access, %	86	
• 6.05 Broadband Internet subscriptions/100 pop	79	
• 6.06 Mobile broadband subscriptions/100 pop	n/a	
• 6.07 Use of virtual social networks*	37	
7th pillar: Business usage		
• 7.01 Firm-level technology absorption*	73	
• 7.02 Capacity for innovation*	119	
• 7.03 PCT patents, applications/million pop	119	
• 7.04 Extent of business Internet use*	74	
• 7.05 Extent of staff training*	32	
8th pillar: Government usage		
• 8.01 Gov't prioritization of ICT*	62	
• 8.02 Importance of ICT to gov't vision*	59	
• 8.03 Government Online Service Index, 0–1 (best)	73	

(continued)

(continued)

9th pillar: Economic impacts		
• 9.01 Impact of ICT on new services and products*	76	
• 9.02 ICT PCT patents, applications/million pop	96	
• 9.03 Impact of ICT on new organizational models*	65	
• 9.04 Knowledge-intensive jobs, % workforce	n/a	
10th pillar: Social impacts		
• 10.01 Impact of ICT on access to basic services*	88	
• 10.02 Internet access in schools*	57	
• 10.03 ICT use and gov't efficiency*	59	
• 10.04 E-Participation Index, 0–1 (best)	79	

© 2012 World Economic Forum

Note: Indicators followed by an (*asterisk*, *) are measured on a 1–7 (best) scale. For further details and explanation, please refer to the section "How to Read the Country/Economy Profiles" on page 171

Data About e-Readiness in Albania According to Global Information Technology Report 2011

Key indicators		
Population (millions), 2009	3.2	12.2
GDP (PPP) per capita (PPP $), 2009	7,169 GDP (US$ billions), 2009	
Global Competitiveness Index 2010–2011 rank (out of 139) 88		

Networked Readiness Index			
Edition	No. of economies	Score	Rank
2010–2011	138	3.6	87
2009–2010	133	3.3	95
2008–2009	134	3.2	105
2007–2008	127	3.1	108
2006–2007	122	2.9	17

162 Environment component 3.5 95		
Market environment 3.9 92		
1.01 Venture capital availability[a]	2.1	106
1.02 Financial market sophistication[a]	3.1	115
1.03 Availability of latest technologies[a]	4.6	89
1.04 State of cluster development[a]	2.6	122
1.05 Burden of government regulation[a]	4.0	19
1.06 Extent and effect of taxation[a]	3.8	39
1.07 Total tax rate, % profits	40.6	69
1.08 No. of days to start a business	5	8

(continued)

(continued)

1.09 No. of procedures to start a business	5	22
1.10 Freedom of the press[a]	4.2	100
Political and regulatory environment 3.8 83		
2.01 Effectiveness of law-making bodies[a]	4.0	41
2.02 Laws relating to ICT[a]	3.9	72
2.03 Judicial independence[a]	3.3	87
2.04 Efficiency of legal system in settling disputes[a]	3.8	58
2.05 Efficiency of legal system in challenging regs[a]	3.8	55
2.06 Property rights[a]	3.3	115
2.07 Intellectual property protection[a]	2.8	100
2.08 Software piracy rate, % software installed	75	76
2.09 No. of procedures to enforce a contract	39	83
2.10 No. of days to enforce a contract	390	26
2.11 Internet and telephony competition, 0–6 (best)	4	85
Infrastructure environment 2.8 98		
3.01 Phone lines/100 pop	11.5	88
3.02 Mobile network coverage, % pop. covered	99.3	46
3.03 Secure Internet servers/million pop	7.0	87
3.04 Int'l Internet bandwidth, Mb/s per 10,000 pop	19.0	59
3.05 Electricity production, kWh/capita	913.0	96
3.06 Tertiary education enrollment rate, %	19.3	90
3.07 Quality scientific research institutions[a]	2.5	127
3.08 Availability of scientists and engineers[a]	3.1	123
3.09 Availability research and training services[a]	3.6	94
3.10 Accessibility of digital content[a]	4.3	101
The Global Information Technology Report 2010–2011 © 2011 World Economic Forum		
Readiness component 4.0 89		
Individual readiness 4.8 78		
4.01 Quality of math and science education[a]	4.2	62
4.02 Quality of educational system[a]	3.9	54
4.03 Adult literacy rate, %	99.0	14
4.04 Residential phone installation (PPP $)	162.1	119
4.05 Residential monthly phone subscription (PPP $)	8.3	46
4.06 Fixed phone tariffs (PPP $)	0.17	78
4.07 Mobile cellular tariffs (PPP $)	0.50	93
4.08 Fixed broadband Internet tariffs (PPP $)	46.3	84
4.09 Buyer sophistication[a]	3.1	98
Business readiness 3.2 127		
5.01 Extent of staff training[a]	4.2	54
5.02 Quality of management schools[a]	3.8	85
5.03 Company spending on R&D[a]	2.7	90
5.04 University-industry collaboration in R&D[a]	2.2	137
5.05 Business phone installation (PPP $)	162.1	106

(continued)

(continued)

5.06 Business monthly phone subscription (PPP $)	31.3	121
5.07 Local supplier quality[a]	3.9	109
5.08 Computer, communications, and other services imports, % services imports	8.9	117
Government readiness 4.1 72		
6.01 Gov't prioritization of ICT[a]	4.5	81
6.02 Gov't procurement of advanced tech[a]	3.7	62
6.03 Importance of ICT to gov't vision[a]	4.0	67
Usage component 3.2 79		
Individual usage 3.5 66		
7.01 Mobile phone subscriptions/100 pop	131.9	22
7.02 Cellular subscriptions w/data, % total	0.0	110
7.03 Households w/personal computer, %	12.0	98
7.04 Broadband Internet subscribers/100 pop	2.9	78
7.05 Internet users/100 pop	41.2	56
7.06 Internet access in schools[a]	3.8	69
7.07 Use of virtual social networks[a]	5.7	34
7.08 Impact of ICT on access to basic services[a]	4.3	75
Business usage 2.8 86		
8.01 Firm-level technology absorption[a]	4.4	91
8.02 Capacity for innovation[a]	2.6	100
8.03 Extent of business Internet use[a]	4.5	94
8.04 National office patent applications/million pop	n/a	n/a
8.05 Patent Cooperation Treaty apps/million pop	0.3	76
8.06 High-tech exports, % goods exports	0.9	83
8.07 Impact of ICT on new services and products[a]	4.5	67
8.08 Impact of ICT on new organizational models[a]	4.4	53
Government usage 3.2 83		
9.01 Gov't success in ICT promotion	3.9	94
9.02 ICT use and gov't efficiency[a]	4.2	73
9.03 Government Online Service Index, 0–1 (best)	0.31	73
9.04 E-Participation Index, 0–1 (best)	0.13	80

[a]Out of a 1–7 (best) scale. This indicator is derived from the World Economic Forum's Executive Opinion Survey

Note: For further details and explanation, please refer to the section "How to Read the Country/Economy Profiles" on page 159

Annex 2

Testing variables with SPSS 17

Test I: Number of Students, Investments, FDI, Internet Bandwidth, Where the Number of Students is the Most Important

Coefficients[a]

Model		Unstandardized coefficients		Standardized coefficients	t	Sig.
		B	Std. error	Beta		
1	(Constant)	7,237.369	0.000		.	.
	Number of students in ICT field	3.930	0.000	1.000	.	.

[a]Dependent variable: total revenues of ICT sector

Test 2

Revenues in ICT with variables of the human factors: enrolment rates, secondary and tertiary, number of students in ICT, and Internet users.

The same exclusions are with the dependent variable of market value of ICT: the most important indicator remains the percentage of Internet users.

© The Author(s) 2015

E. Kordha Tolica et al., *Information Society Development through ICT Market Strategies*, SpringerBriefs in Business, DOI 10.1007/978-3-319-17196-8

Coefficients[a]

Model		Unstandardized coefficients	Standardized coefficients			
		B	Std. Error	Beta	t	Sig.
1	(Constant)	12,150.741	0.000		.	.
	Percentage of Internet users	286.054	0.000	1.000	.	.

[a]Dependent variable: total revenues of ICT sector

Excluded variables[b]

Model		Beta In	T	Sig.	Partial correlation	Collinearity statistics Tolerance
1	Number of students in ICT field	[a]	.	.	.	0.000
	Gross secondary enrolment rate	[a]	.	.	.	0.000
	Gross tertiary enrolment rate	[a]	.	.	.	0.000

[a]Predictors in the Model: (Constant), percentage of Internet users
[b]Dependent variable: total revenues of ICT sector

Test 3

The three variables of entrepreneurship with revenues and with market value show that lending level of economy and investments in telecommunications are excluded.

Coefficients[a]

Model		Unstandardized coefficients	Standardized coefficients			
		B	Std. Error	Beta	t	Sig.
1	(Constant)	23,283.750	0.000		.	.
	FDI in communications	−12.310	0.000	−1.000	.	.

[a]Dependent variable: total revenues of ICT sector

Excluded variables[b]

Model		Beta In	T	Sig.	Partial Correlation	Collinearity Statistics Tolerance
1	Investments commitments of telecommunications	.[a]	.	.	.	0.000
	Lending level of economy	.[a]	.	.	.	0.000

[a]Predictors in the model: (Constant), FDI in communications
[b]Dependent variable: total revenues of ICT sector

Test 4

Infrastructure and access factors, the most important ones have been percentage of households with computers and mobile subscriptions, while fixed subscriptions, Internet bandwidth, and households with Internet access have been excluded.

Coefficients[a]

Model		Unstandardized coefficients		Standardized coefficients			
		B	Std. error	Beta	t	Sig.
1	(Constant)	−88,466.965	0.000		.	.
	Mobile subscriptions /100 inhabitants	735.670	0.000	0.415	.	.
	Percentage of Households with computer	5,370.253	0.000	0.723	.	.

[a]Dependent variable: total revenues of ICT sector

The most important is the percentage of households with computer: it is understood from the beta coefficients.

Test 5

FDI in communications, government expenditures, Internet bandwidth, Investments commitments,

Coefficients[a]

Model		Unstandardized coefficients		Standardized coefficients			
		B	Std. error	Beta	t	Sig.
1	(Constant)	23,283.750	0.000		.	.
	FDI in communications	−12.310	0.000	−1.000	.	.

[a]Dependent variable: total revenues of ICT sector

Excluded variables[b]

Model		Beta In	T	Sig.	Partial correlation	Collinearity statistics Tolerance
1	GOV expenditures in ICT	.[a]	.	.	.	0.000
	Internet bandwidth (bit/Internet user)	.[a]	.	.	.	0.000
	Investments commitments of telecommunications	.[a]	.	.	.	0.000

[a]Predictors in the Model: (Constant), FDI in communications
[b]Dependent variable: total revenues of ICT sector

Test 6

The test included the most important variables that were identified in the first phase of SPSS testing for variables within each category. As mentioned above, they were the Government expenditures in ICT, Percentage of Internet users, mobile subscriptions for 100 inhabitants, Percentage of households with computers and FDI in communications. The testing shows that the predictors of the model are Government expenditures in ICT and Mobile subscriptions for 100 inhabitants. The most important is mobile subscriptions per 100 inhabitants.

Coefficients[a]

Model		Unstandardized coefficients		Standardized coefficients	t	Sig.
		B	Std. error	Beta		
1	(Constant)	−179,125.504	0.000	.	.	.
	GOV expenditures in ICT	0.340	0.000	0.622	.	.
	Mobile subscriptions /100 inhabitants	1,341.804	0.000	0.756	.	.

[a]Dependent variable: total revenues of ICT sector

Another test is that of dependent variable market value of ICT which shows that the most important indicator is the percentage of households with computer, than FDI in communications than government expenditures in ICT. The human factor has not been a very important element in the development of ICT sector, while the infrastructure has been the most important one.

Coefficients[a]

Model		Unstandardized coefficients		Standardized coefficients	t	Sig.
		B	Std. error	Beta		
1	(Constant)	−558,138.049	0.000		.	.
	GOV expenditures in ICT	1.518	0.000	3.498	.	.
	Percentage of Internet users	−4,184.480	0.000	−3.680	.	.
	FDI in communications	251.573	0.000	1.447	.	.
	Percentage of Households with computer	13,025.817	0.000	2.183	.	.

[a]Dependent variable: market value of ICT

Bibliography

Audenhove, L.V., (2000). Information and communication technology policy in Africa: A critical analysis of rhetoric and practice. In: C. AVGEROU and G. WALSHAM, eds, Burlington, USA: Ashgate Publishing company, pp. 277–290.

Avgerou, C. and Walsham, G., (2000). Introduction: IT in developing countries. In: C. AVGEROU and G. WALSHAM, eds, *Information technology in context: Studies from the perspective of developing countries.* 1 edn. Burlington, USA: Ashgate Publishing company, pp. 1–7.

Al-Qirim, NAY (Ed.) (2004). Electronic commerce in small to medium-sized enterprises: Frameworks, issues, and implications, Idea Group, Hershey, PA.

Bar & Park, 2006 Bar, F., and Park, N. (2006). Perspectiva Global. Lisbon, Portugal. Municipal Wi-Fi Networks: The Goals, Practices, and Policy.

Bell, 1973; Bell, D. (1973). *The coming of post-industrial society: A venture in social forecasting.* New York: Basic Books.

Bakry, (2003). Development of security policies for private networks, International Journal of Network Management, Volume 13, Issue 3, pages 203–210, May/June 2003.

Bleha, T. (2005). Down to the Wire. Foreign Affairs, 84(3), 111–124.

Bridges.org (2005). eReady For What? E-Readiness in Developing countries: Current status and Prospects toward the Millenium Development Goals. http://www.infodev.org/files/2049_file_InforDev_E_Rdnss_Rpt_rev11May05.pdf

Bridges, 2001 Comparison of E-readiness assessment Models http://insme.org/documenti/Bennister.pdf

Brown, R. H., Irving, L., Prabhakar, A., & Katzen, S. (1995). The Global Information Infrastructure: Agenda for Cooperation: Information Infrastructure Task Force.

Bar, F., & Galperin, H. (2005). Geeks, Cowboys and Bureaucrats: Deploying Broadband, the Wireless Way, A Sociedade em Rede e a Economia do Conhecimento: Portugal numa Perspectiva Global. Lisbon, Portugal.

Buck, S. (2002). Replacing Spectrum Auction with a Spectrum Commons. Stanford Technology Law Review, 2.

Bartelsman and Doms, (2000). "Understanding Productivity: Lessons from Longi- tudinal Micro Datasets", *Journal of Economic Literature*, Vol. 38, September.

Bresnahan and Greenstein (1996). "Technical Progress and Co-Invention in Computing and the Use of Computers", *Brookings Papers on Economic Activity: Microeconomics*, pp. 1–77.

Bharati, P. and Chaudhury, A. (2006). "Current status of technology adoption: Micro, small and-medium manufacturing firms in Boston", Communications of the ACM, vol. 49, no. 10, pp. 88–93.

© The Author(s) 2015
E. Kordha Tolica et al., *Information Society Development through ICT Market Strategies*, SpringerBriefs in Business, DOI 10.1007/978-3-319-17196-8

Belson, K. (2006, 26 June). What If They Built an Urban Wireless Network and Hardly Anyone Used It? New York Times, p. C1.

Caldeira, M.M. and Ward, J.M. (2003) 'Using resource-based theory to interpret the successful adoption and use of information systems and technology in manufacturing small and medium-sized enterprises', European Journal of Information Systems, 12(2), pp. 127–141.

Castells, M. (1989). The Informational City: Information Technology, Economic Restructuring, and the Urban-Regional Process. Oxford, UK ; Cambridge, Mass., USA: B. Blackwell.

Castells, M. (1996). *The information age: Economy, society and culture. The rise of network society* (Vol. 1). Oxford: Blackwell Publishers.

Castells, M. (1997). *The information age: Economy, society and culture. The rise of network society.* (Vol. 2). Oxford: Blackwell Publishers.

Castells, M. (1998). *The information age: Economy, society and culture. The rise of network society.* (Vol. 3). Oxford: Blackwell Publishers.

Caves, R. W., & Walshok, M. G. (1999). Adopting Innovations in Information Technology: The California Municipal Experience. Cities, 16(1), 3–12.

Cayla, G., Cohen, S. & Guigon, D. (2005). Wimax - an efficient tool to bridge the digital divide. WiMAX Forum. November, 2005 Retrieved from http://www.wimaxforum.org/news/down-loads/WiMAX_to_Bridge_the_Digitaldivid e.pdf

Cellary, W. (2002). Jak uniknąć wykluczenia w społeczeństwie informacyjnym. In *Raport: Polska w drodze do globalnego społeczeństwa informacyjnego*, Poznań.

Chan, C. B2B E-Commerce Stages of Growth: the strategic imperatives/Chan C.; Swatman P.M.C. Proceedings of Conference 'HICSS-37' - 37th Hawaii International Conference on System Sciences, Hawaii, USA, January 5–8, 2004.

Chinn, Menzie D., Robert W. Fairlie. (2001). "The Determinants of the Global Digital Divide: A Cross-Country Analysis of Computer and Internet, Ibid.

CID, 2006 Readiness for the Networked World – A guide for Developing Countries, http://www.readinessguide.com

Cogburn D. L. and Adeya C. N.,1999, Globalization and the Information Economy: Challenges and opportunities for Africa. United Nations Economic Commission

Cracin (2005). Written Submission to Telecommunications Policy Review Panel. Toronto: Canadian Research Alliance for Community Innovation & Networking.

CRTC. (2006). Broadcasting Policy Monitoring Report. Ottawa.

Drucker, Drucker, P. F. (1993). *Post-capitalist society.* New York: Harper Business. *Final report for the thematic evaluation of the information society.* (2002). Technopolis Ltd. IRISI Europe. http://ec.europa.eu/regional_policy/sources/docgener/evaluation/doc/information_society.pdf

Ewalt, D. M. (2005). Orlando Kills Municipal Wi-Fi Project. Retrieved 22 September, 2006, from http://www.forbes.com/home/technology/2005/06/23/municipal-wifi-failure- cx_de_0623wifi.html

EIU (2010). Digital Economy Rankings 2010, beyond e-readiness, a report from the Economist Intelligence Unit, retrieved from http://graphics.eiu.com/upload/EIU_Digital_economy_rank-ings_2010_FINAL_WEB.pdf

EIU (2012). Digital Economy Rankings 2012, beyond e-readiness, a report from the Economist Intelligence Unit.

Fransman, M. (2006). Global Broadband Battles: Why the U.S. And Europe Lag While Asia Leads. Stanford: Stanford Business Books.

Feld, H., Rose, G., Cooper, M., & Scott, B. (2005). Connecting the Public: The Truth About Municipal Broadband. Washington, D.C.: Consumer Federation of American, Consumers Union.

Fuentes-Bautista, M., & Inagaki, N. (2005). The Wi-Fi's Promise and Broadband Divides: Reconfiguring Public Internet Access in Austin, Texas. Paper presented at the Telecommunication Policy Research Conference, Arlington, VA.

Fichman, R.G. (2000). The diffusion and assimilation of information technology innovations. In Zmud R.W., (Ed.), Framing the domains of IT management: Projecting the future through the past. Cincinnati: Pinnaflex Education Resources.

Galperin (2005) Galperin, H. (2005). Wireless Networks and Rural Development: Opportunities for Latin America. Information Technologies and International Development, 2(3), 47–56.

Gatautis R (2008). Information technology in context: Studies from the perspective of developing countries. 1 edn. Burlington, USA: Ashgate Publishing company, pp. 1-7. ENGINEERING ECONOMICS. 2008. No 4 (59)

Gichoya D (2005). "Factors Affecting the Successful Implementation of ICT Projects in Government" *The Electronic Journal of e-Government* Volume 3 Issue 4, pp 175-184, available online at www.ejeg.com

Garfield (2001). An Information society? Reprinted in Essays of an Information Scientist, Vol:6, p.609–615, 1983

Geist M. (2005, 28 February). Let Towns, Cities Provide Cheap, Everywhere Broadband. Toronto Star.

George Sciadas (2005). From the Digital Divide to Digital Opportunities. Measuring Infostates for Development, Orbicom and ITU.

Giovannini E, and Uysal A. (2006). OECD workshop on business and consumer tendency surveys, Statistics, Knowledge and Policy: What Do We Know About What People Know?, Statistics Directorate OECD.

Gillett, S. E. (2006). Municipal Wireless Broadband: Hype or Harbinger? Southern California Law Review, 79, 561–594.

Gillett, S. E., Lehr, W. H., & Osorio, C. (2004). Local Government Broadband Initiatives. Telecommunications Policy, 28(7–8), 537–558.

Gillett, S. E., Lehr, W. H., & Osorio, C. A. (2006a). Municipal Electric Utilities' Role in Telecommunications Services. Telecommunications Policy, 30(8–9), 464–480.

Gillett, S. E., Lehr, W. H., Osorio, C. A., & Sirbu, M. A. (2006b). Measuring Broadband's Economic Impact: Final Report. Washington, DC: U.S. Department of Commerce, Economic Development Administration.

Gurumurthy and Singh 2005 *Gurumurthy A., and Singh, P.J, 2005,* Political Economy of the Information Society A Southern View Available at WSISPapers.Choike.org

Heeks, R., (2002). Information Systems and Developing countries: Failure, success, and local improvisations.   http://www.fes.uwaterloo.ca/crs/plan674d/isysanddcountries.pdf   edn. Philadelphia: Taylor & Francis.

Horrigan, J. B. (2006). Home Broadband Adoption 2006. Washington, DC: Pew Internet & American Life Project.

Industry Canada. (2002). Broadband for Rural and Northern Development. Ottawa.

Industry Canada. (2005). Broadband - The Programs - National Satellite Initiative Retrieved from http://broadband.gc.ca/pub/program/nsi/aboutus.html.

Horrigan, J. B. (2006). Home Broadband Adoption 2006. Washington, DC: Pew Internet & American Life Project.

International Telecommunication Union, 2004 International Telecommunication Union. (2004). The Portable Internet. Geneva: ITU.

International Telecommunication Union, ITU 2005, Measuring Digital Opportunity ITU/Korea WSIS Thematic Meeting on Multistakeholder Partnerships for Bridging the Digital Divide, Seoul Republic of Korea, 23–24 June 2005.

ITU (2007), *Telecommunication Indicators Handbook*, http://www.itu.int/ITU-D/ict/handbook. html.

Information Highway Advisory Council. (1997). Preparing Canada for a Digital World: Final Report of the Information Highway Advisory Council. Ottawa.

Industry Canada. Infrastructure Canada. (2004). Enhancing Knowledge About Public Infrastructure: Perspectives in the Federal Family Report. Ottawa.

Yun–Hwan Kim, (2000). Financing Information Technology Diffusion in Low–income Asian Developing Countries, Journal of Asian development, 115–133.

Karvalics, Z. L. (1997). Az információstratégiák kialakulása és jellemzői. Magyarország esélyei és lehetőségei különös tekintettel az EU-integrációra. [Emergence and characteristics of information strategies. Chances and possibilities of Hungary with special reference to the EU-integration], *Available from*: www.tar.hu/isip/itip/ZKL_infstrat_miajovo.doc

Karvalics, Z. L. (2005). Információ, tudás, társadalom, gazdaság, technológia: egy egységes terminológia felé. [Information, knowledge, society, economy, technology: towards a unified terminologyg] *Információs Társadalom*, Vol. 4., 7–17., ISSN 1587–8694.

Lihtenberg F. R. (1995). "The Output Contributions of Computer Equipment and Personal: A Firm–level Analysis", Economics of Innovation and New Technology, 3.

Lehr, W., & McKnight, L. W. (2003). Wireless Internet Access: 3G vs. WiFi Telecommunications Policy, 27, 351–370.

Mackenzie, A. (2005). Untangling the Unwired: Wi-Fi and the Cultural Inversion of Infrastructure. Space and Culture, 8(3), 269–285.

Markle Foundation, (2003), *Global Digital Opportunities: National Strategies of "ICT for Development"*.

Mansell, R., & Steinmuller, W. E. (2000). *Mobilizing the information society. Strategies for growth and opportunity*. Oxford: Oxford University Press.

Mgaya, R.J., (1999). *Adoption and diffusion of group support systems in Tanzania*, Delft University of Technology.

Maugis V, Chouci, N., Madnick, S., Siegel, M., Gillet S., Hughseta, F., Zhu, H and Best M. (2005). Global e-Readiness – for What? Readiness for e-banking, Information Technology Readiness for Development, 11, 4, 313–342

Meinrath, S. (2005). Community Wireless Networking and Open Spectrum Usage: A Research Agenda to Support Progressive Policy Reform of the Public Airwaves. The Journal of Community Informatics, 1(2).

Middleton, C. A., & Sorensen, C. (2005). How Connected Are Canadians? Inequities in Canadian Households' Internet Access. Canadian Journal of Communication, 30(4), 463–483.

National Broadband Task Force. (2001). The New National Dream: Networking the Nation for Broadband Access. Ottawa: Industry Canada.

New Millennium Research Council. (2005). Not in The Public Interest – The Myth of Municipal Wi-Fi Networks: Why Municipal Schemes to Provide Wi-Fi Broadband Service with Public Funds Are Ill-Advised. Washington, DC.

Odedra, M., (1993). IT policies in the commonwealth developing countries. In: G. HARINDRANATH and J. LIEBENAU, eds, *Information technology policies and applications in the commonwealth countries*. 1 edn. London: Commonwealth secretariat, pp. 9–35.

Olszak, C. M., &Ziemba, E. (2008). The conceptual model of a web learning portal for small and medium sized enterprises. *Issues in Informing Science and Information Technology. Informing Science Institute*, 5, 335-351. Retrieved from; http://iisit.org/IssuesVol5.htm

OECD, (2003) *ICT and economic growth: Evidence from OECD countries, industries and firms*.

Organisation for Economic Co-Operation and Development. (2006). OECD Broadband Statistics, December 2005. Retrieved 31 July, 2006, from http://www.oecd.org/document/39/0,2340, en_2825_495656_36459431_1_1_1_1,00.ht ml.

Peters, T. (2003). Bridging the Digital Divide. 28-31. Retrieved from http://www.ciaonet.org/olj/gli/gli_nov2003/gli_nov2003h.pdf

Powell, A., & Shade, L. R. (2006). Going Wi-Fi in Canada: Municipal and community initiatives. Government Information Quarterly, 23(3-4), 381–403.

Prabhakar, & Katzen, 1995;

Sandvig, C. (2004). An Initial Assessment of Cooperative Action in Wi-Fi Networking. Telecommunications Policy, 28(7/8), 579–602.

Schuler, D., & Day, P. (2004). Shaping the Network Society: The New Role of Civil Society in Cyberspace. Cambridge, Mass.: MIT Press.

Strover, S., Chapman, G., & Waters, J. (2003). Beyond Community Networking and CTCs: Access, Development and Public Policy. Paper presented at the Telecommunication Policy Research Conference, Arlington, VA.

Sassen, S. (2002). Global Networks, Linked Cities. New York: Routledge.

Servon, L. J. (2002). Bridging the Digital Divide: Technology, Community, and Public Policy. Malden, MA: Blackwell Pub.

Sevrani, K., Malolli, I., Measurement of e-services, factors that can improve the e-government, e-participation, Journal "Science, Innovation and New Technology" 01/2011; Vol 1(Issue 1)

Sandvig, C., (2004). An initial assessment of cooperative action in Wi-Fi networking. Telecommunications Policy 28, 579–602.

Sawhney, H., (2003). Wi-Fi networks and the rerun of the cycle. info 5, 25–33.

Shamp, S. A. (2004). Wi-Fi Clouds and Zones: A Survey of Municipal Wireless Initiatives: Mobile Media Consortium, University of Georgia.

Telecommunications Policy Review Panel, (2006). Telecommunications Policy Review Panel - Final Report 2006. Ottawa: Industry Canada.

Tapia, A. H., Stone, M., & Maitland, C. (2005). Public-Private Partnerships and the Role of State and Federal Legislation in Wireless Municipal Networks. Paper presented at the Telecommunication Policy Research Conference, Arlington, VA.

Toffler, A. (1980). *The third wave*. New York: Bantam Books.

Van Ark and Inklaar 2005

Vos, E. (2005). Muniwireless.Com July 2005 Report.

UN report (2003). UNDESA team and Civic Resource Group. (2003). UN Global E-Government Survey report 2003.

Warschauer, M. (2003). Technology and Social Inclusion: Rethinking the Digital Divide. Cambridge, Mass.: MIT Press.

Westrup, C., (2002). What's in information technology? Issues in deploying IS in organisations and developing countries. In: C. Avgerou and G. Walsham, eds, *Information technology in context: Studies from the perspective of developing countries*. Burlington, USA: Ashgate publishing company, pp. 96–110.

Wilhelm, A. G. (2004). Digital Nation: Toward an Inclusive Information Society. Cambridge: MIT Press.